Contents

KT-498-312

Getting the most from this book

Questions & Answers

Exam-style questions

Examiner comments on the questions
Tips on what you need to do to gain full marks, indicated by the icon ⓔ.

Sample student answers
Practise the questions, then look at the student answers that follow each set of questions.

Examiner commentary on sample student answers
Find out how many marks each answer would be awarded in the exam and then read the examiner comments (preceded by the icon ⓔ) following each student answer. Annotations that link back to points made in the student answers show exactly how and where marks are gained or lost.

STUDENT UNIT GUIDE

NEW EDITION

AQA AS Economics Unit 1
Markets and Market Failure

Ray Powell

 PHILIP ALLAN

Philip Allan Updates, an imprint of Hodder Education, an Hachette UK company, Market Place, Deddington, Oxfordshire OX15 0SE

Orders
Bookpoint Ltd, 130 Milton Park, Abingdon, Oxfordshire, OX14 4SB
tel: 01235 827827
fax: 01235 400401
e-mail: uk.orders@bookpoint.co.uk
Lines are open 9.00 a.m.–5.00 p.m., Monday to Saturday, with a 24-hour message answering service. You can also order through the Philip Allan Updates website: www.philipallan.co.uk

ISBN 978-1-4441-4824-4

First printed 2011
Impression number 5 4 3
Year 2015 2014 2013 2012

Printed in Dubai

Hachette UK's policy is to use papers that are natural, renewable and recyclable products and made from wood grown in sustainable forests. The logging and manufacturing processes are expected to conform to the environmental regulations of the country of origin.

P01927

About this book

The aim of this Guide is to prepare students for the AQA Advanced Subsidiary ECON 1 examination assessing **Unit 1: Markets and Market Failure**.

Content Guidance

Start off by reading the Content Guidance section of the book, which divides the Unit 1 specification into nine separate topics. You can read all the topics, one by one, before proceeding to the Questions and Answers section of the Guide. Alternatively, you may decide to read a particular topic and then to read the corresponding part of the Questions and Answers section. The topics follow the order of the Unit 1 specification, proceeding from markets through market failure and then on to government intervention in markets in order to correct market failure.

Questions and Answers

You should read the Questions and Answers section of the book either after reading all nine specification topics in the Content Guidance section, or bit by bit, having revised a selected topic on a particular part of the specification.

Objective-test questions (OTQs)

There are nineteen **objective-test questions (OTQs)** and six **data-response questions (DRQs)** in the Questions and Answers section of the Guide. The OTQs divide into two parts. The first OTQs are questions typical of those commonly set on each of the nine topics covered in the Content Guidance section of the Guide. Each of these questions is similar in layout, structure and style to an OTQ in the ECON 1 examination paper. A commentary has been included after each question to explain the correct answer and any other important features of the question. These questions are then followed by ten OTQs, chosen to represent the types of question that regularly catch out unwary students. For these questions, the commentary after each question explains the nature of the pitfall that may catch you out.

Data-response questions (DRQs)

The nineteen OTQs are followed by six data-response questions. You can use the DRQs either as timed test questions in the lead-up to the examination or to reinforce your understanding of the specification subject matter, topic by topic, as you proceed through the Content Guidance. In this Guide, the data-response questions are numbered 1 to 6, but in the AQA exam you will eventually sit, the two questions will be numbered Context 1 and Context 2.

This section, covering the data-response questions, also includes:
- A student's answer for each DRQ.
- Examiner's comments on each student's answer explaining, where relevant, how the answer could be improved. These comments are denoted by the icon ⓔ.

Using other economics resources

This Guide should be used as a supplement to other resources, such as class notes, textbooks, *Economic Review* magazine and *AS/A-Level Economics Exam Revision Notes*. (The last two of these are published by Philip Allan Updates.) As this Guide contains summaries rather than in-depth coverage of all the topics in the specification, you should not use the Guide as your sole learning resource during the main part of the course. However, you may well decide to use the Guide as the key resource in your revision programme. You are strongly advised to make full use of the Questions and Answers section, especially in the revision period when you should be concentrating on improving your examination skills.

Content guidance

Summary of the specification

The AQA specification for Markets and Market Failure contains the following sections.

3.1.1 The economic problem

How can you decide whether a market performs well or badly? You must assess the extent to which the market contributes to the solution of the economic problem, which is the title of both the first section of the specification and the first topic in this Guide. A market performs well when the price mechanism, operating within the market, solves to a satisfactory degree the economic problem of scarcity. By contrast, if the price mechanism (or market mechanism) functions unsatisfactorily (or, in extreme cases, breaks down completely and fails to function at all), market failure occurs. Some resources which appear to be 'free' and available in unlimited supply are in fact scarce. The environment is an example of such a scarce resource, and its scarcity is affected by many of the economic decisions made by human beings.

The central purpose of economic activity is to improve **economic welfare** (which can be thought of as happiness enjoyed by the whole population). For the most part, improving economic welfare requires production of goods and services so that people's needs and wants can be satisfied. The production of goods and services in turn means that questions have to be addressed such as what to produce, how to produce and for whom to produce.

The key concepts you must know which relate to the economic problem of scarcity are: the nature of **economic resources** or **factors of production** (land, labour, capital and enterprise); the importance of **choice** and **opportunity cost**; and the assumption that all **economic agents** (households, firms and the government) have **objectives** that they wish to maximise. You must also understand the difference between free goods and economic goods. **Production possibility curve** diagrams (which also figure in specification section 3.1.3 in relation to the key concept of economic efficiency) can be used to illustrate the economic problem and two other key concepts in section 3.1.1: **opportunity cost** and the **trade-off** between conflicting objectives. Finally, this section of the specification requires that you recognise **value judgements** and understand the difference between **positive statements** (statements of fact or statements that can be shown to be either true or false) and **normative statements** (statements of opinion). You must also familiarise yourself with the role incentives play in economic activity and in providing satisfactory answers to questions such as those outlined in the previous paragraph.

3.1.2 The allocation of resources in competitive markets

This is the core area of the specification, at the centre of which is the supply and demand economic model. To meet the requirements of this section of the specification, you must learn, understand and be able to apply important terms and concepts such as demand, supply, equilibrium, disequilibrium and elasticity, and the signalling, incentive and rationing functions of prices. Make sure you can apply elasticity formulae to calculate price elasticity of demand, income elasticity of demand, cross elasticity of demand and price elasticity of supply. You must understand the difference between a shift of a demand or supply curve and an adjustment along a supply or demand curve in response to a price change. Practise drawing supply and demand diagrams to illustrate shifts of supply and demand caused by changes in factors, other than price, which determine supply and demand. You must learn to apply your knowledge of the basic model of demand and supply to markets, including commodity markets such as oil and copper markets, agriculture, healthcare, housing, sport and leisure.

Probably the most important skill you must learn when studying this section of the specification is **applying demand and supply analysis to particular markets**. This is a key skill tested in the Unit 1 examination – one of the two data-response questions is likely to be set on a **primary product** or **industrial market**.

3.1.3 Production and efficiency

As already mentioned, throughout your studies you must always remember that improved economic welfare is the ultimate purpose of economic activity, but that production of more goods and services is usually necessary for welfare to increase. In order to maximise welfare, production must take place efficiently rather than inefficiently. You must understand and learn to apply the concept of productive efficiency, which involves maximising output of goods and services from available inputs (the economic resources or factors of production mentioned in section 3.1.1).

Two factors that increase productive efficiency are **specialisation** and **economies of scale**. Specialisation, which occurs when different industries produce different goods and services, leads to the growth of **trade** and **exchange**. Economies of scale, which result from the growth in size of firms and industries, lead to falling average costs of production and to an increase in productive efficiency. By contrast, **diseconomies of scale**, which involve rising average costs as the scale of a firm increases, result in productive inefficiency. Diseconomies of scale discourage any further growth of a firm. For a firm, **productive efficiency** occurs when economies of scale have been achieved to the full, but before diseconomies of scale cause average costs to rise.

The economy as a whole is productively efficient when production takes place on the economy's **production possibility frontier** or boundary. In this situation, it is impossible to increase production of one good without reducing production of one or more other goods.

3.1.4 Market failure

Market failure occurs whenever markets perform badly or unsatisfactorily. Markets may fail either because they perform inequitably (unfairly or unjustly) or because they perform inefficiently. Different people have different opinions about what is fair, so the first type of market failure depends on normative views or value judgements (see section 3.1.1).

Many economists argue that **inequalities in the distributions of income and wealth** provide a significant example of market failure resulting from markets performing inequitably. Whenever markets are productively inefficient (a key concept in section 3.1.3), or when they misallocate resources between competing uses, the second type of market failure occurs. **Monopoly** is an important example. If the **incentive function of prices** (see section 3.1.2) breaks down completely, markets may be unable to produce any quantity of a good. **Public goods** provide an example, and there are also **'missing markets'** in **externalities**. In other cases, markets may succeed in providing a good, but end up providing the 'wrong' quantity. This happens if the market price is too high, which discourages consumption, or too low, which has the opposite effect of encouraging too much consumption. The main examples are **merit** and **demerit goods**.

You must practise drawing diagrams to show the **marginal private, external**, and **social cost** and **benefit curves** relevant to externalities and merit and demerit goods. You should be able to illustrate the misallocation of resources resulting. These diagrams should be used to illustrate the difference between the **privately optimal** and the **socially optimal** levels of goods when externalities are generated in the course of either production or consumption — and the associated **resource misallocation**. Students should also understand that the classification of merit and demerit goods depends upon value judgements and that production of merit and demerit goods may be subject to positive and negative externalities in consumption. Under-provision of merit goods, and over-provision of demerit goods, may also result from imperfect information.

Monopoly should also be treated as an example of a market failure, which in the absence of economies of scale, results in productive inefficiency and a misallocation of resources compared to the outcome in a competitive market. You must understand that many real-world markets display evidence of market power, even when there is more than one firm. **Barriers to entry** and the degree of **market concentration** and **product differentiation** should be appreciated as sources of monopoly power. Nevertheless, you should also be aware of the potential benefits of monopoly: for example, economies of scale and possibly more invention and innovation.

Immobility of factors of production is also likely to lead to a misallocation of resources and therefore cause market failure.

3.1.5 Government intervention in the market

When studying government intervention, you should distinguish between the government's objectives and the methods it uses to achieve its objectives. Section 3.1.1 introduced one of the most important assumptions in economics — that every economic agent has an objective that it tries to achieve and maximise. When analysing the role of the state in the economy, economists usually assume that governments wish to maximise the public interest or social welfare (i.e. the economic welfare of the whole community).

When intervening in the market, governments have various **policy instruments** at their disposal. The most extreme method of intervention involves **abolishing the market**, such as when the government **provides public and merit goods directly** and finances their provision through the tax system. At the other extreme, governments often allow markets to function largely free of intervention, but modified to some extent by the effect of taxes or minor regulation. **Taxation** and **regulation** provide the main forms of government intervention in markets. Other methods of intervention cited in the specification include **subsidies**, **price controls** and in the case of negative externalities, **permits to pollute**.

You might also be asked to explain, analyse and assess the effectiveness of intervention in the form of **buffer stock schemes** or **price stabilisation policies**: for example, the imposition of **price ceilings** or **price floors**. The specification hints that the **Common Agricultural Policy (CAP)** of the European Union may provide the context for a question on government intervention in agricultural markets. Government intervention in the **transport market** might also figure strongly in a question.

Much government intervention attempts to correct the various market failures outlined in section 3.1.4. However, an attempt to correct market failure can lead to **government failure**. First, government intervention to correct a market failure or to achieve the government's objectives may simply be unsuccessful. Second, and often more seriously, completely new economic problems may emerge as a direct result of government intervention trying to correct other problems.

The economic problem

These notes relate to AQA specification section 3.1.1 and prepare you to answer examination questions on:
- the purpose of economic activity
- the fundamental economic problem of scarcity
- related economic concepts, such as opportunity cost, the conflicts and trade-offs involved when households and firms try to achieve their goals or objectives, and the role of factors of production

Essential information

The purpose of economic activity and the problem of scarcity

Economics is literally the study of economising — the study of how human beings make choices on what to produce, how to produce and for whom to produce, in a world in which most of the resources are limited. Because resources are limited in relation to people's infinite wants, the problem of scarcity is the fundamental economic problem.

The ultimate purpose or objective of **economic activity** is to increase people's happiness or **economic welfare**. Increased production enables economic welfare to increase, but only if the production of more goods and services leads to higher levels of consumption. Production and consumption often lead to resource **depletion** (using up scarce resources) and resource **degradation** (e.g. pollution and destruction of the natural environment).

As a general rule, consumption increases economic welfare and people's standard of living (although in certain circumstances consumption can reduce rather than increase welfare). Economists often use the word **utility** for the welfare that people enjoy when they consume goods and services. Goods such as food bought for consumption are known as **consumer goods**; by contrast, a good such as a machine bought by a firm in order to produce other goods is called a **capital good**. Goods that people produce for their own consumption, and activities such as contemplating the natural environment, contribute to people's utility or welfare, adding to the utility obtained from consuming goods bought in the market.

The economy's production possibility frontier

The production possibility frontier in Figure 1 shows the various possible combinations of capital goods and consumer goods that the economy can produce when all the available inputs or economic resources are being used to the full.

Suppose that initially the economy is at point A on the frontier, producing K_1 capital goods and C_1 consumer goods. In the absence of economic growth (which moves the frontier outwards), consumer good production can only increase to C_2 if the production of capital goods falls from to K_1 to K_2. The fall in the production of capital goods when the production of consumer goods increases is called an opportunity cost.

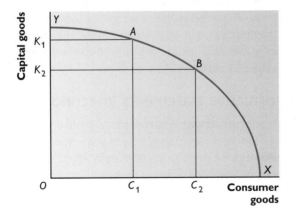

Figure 1 An economy's production possibility frontier

economic problem
Only a limited amount of resources is available to produce the unlimited quantity of goods and services people desire.

opportunity cost The opportunity cost of any decision is the next best alternative sacrificed or given up.

Examiner tip
You must learn to draw and interpret production possibility diagrams, which are very important in the ECON 2 exam as well as in the ECON 1 exam.

Knowledge check 2
Give an example of an opportunity cost, other than the capital goods given up when the production of consumer goods increases.

Maximising behaviour and rational behaviour

Economists usually assume that households and firms (and other **economic agents**, such as the government) have economic objectives that they wish to maximise.

The objectives are generally taken to be:
- profit in the case of producers (or firms)
- utility or consumer welfare for members of households
- the public interest, or social welfare, in the case of governments

Economic behaviour is thus maximising behaviour. Everybody is assumed to be rational, which means that people always try to choose the best possible outcome in preference to the next best.

Trading-off between different objectives

trading-off When two or more objectives conflict with each other and are impossible to achieve simultaneously, a trade-off is a decision to try to achieve the conflicting objectives to a certain extent, but without maximising any of the objectives.

Very often it is difficult to choose between different outcomes that all have advantages and disadvantages. In this situation, it may be possible to resolve the conflict by trading-off between the alternatives. Points A and B in Figure 1 illustrate trading-off. Instead of producing only capital goods (at point Y) or only consumer goods (at point X), combinations of capital and consumer goods can be produced at intermediate points on the frontier, such as A or B. The production of capital goods can be traded-off against the production of consumer goods.

Free goods and economic goods

Most goods and services that add to our economic welfare and contribute to our standard of living have to be produced from scarce resources. (Exceptions, such as sea water for a person living on the coast, are known as **free goods**. As their name implies, free goods are not bought and sold at a price because they are not scarce and because no costs of production are involved.)

Goods other than free goods are examples of **economic goods**. Scarcity and the need to pay a price to obtain the good mean that people have to economise when deciding whether or not to buy an economic good. For a consumer, the opportunity cost of buying an economic good is the other goods that could have been bought instead. Likewise, the production of an economic good involves an opportunity cost — in this case, other goods that the factors of production employed to produce the good could have produced instead.

Positive and normative statements in economics

A lot of economics is concerned with what people *ought* to do. *Ought* the government try to make markets function more fairly? Such a question falls within the remit of **normative economics**. Normative economics is about **value judgements** and **opinions**, but because people have different opinions about what is right and wrong, normative statements cannot be scientifically tested. They are just opinions.

By contrast, a **positive statement** can be scientifically tested to see if it is incorrect. If a positive statement does not pass the test, it is falsified. However, a positive statement does not have to be true. For example, 'the moon is made of green cheese' is a positive statement. A few people may believe it, though obviously with the growth of scientific evidence, the statement has been falsified. The key point is that positive statements can in principle be tested and possibly falsified, while normative statements cannot. Words such as 'ought', 'should', 'better', 'worse' and 'good' and 'bad' (used as adjectives) often provide clues that a statement is normative.

Examination skills

The skills most likely to be tested by objective-test and data-response questions on the economic problem are as follows:
- Interpreting and possibly drawing a production possibility diagram such as Figure 1.
- Understanding and explaining that the purpose of economic activity is to increase welfare.
- Understanding and explaining how the scenario of the question illustrates the problem of scarcity.
- Explaining and applying the concept of opportunity cost.
- Analysing an economic problem in terms of trade-offs between conflicting objectives.
- Distinguishing between a statement of fact (a positive statement) and a value judgement (a normative statement).

Examination questions

Knowledge and understanding of scarcity may be tested by OTQs in the contexts of production possibility frontiers and free goods. Because it is the central topic in economics, virtually every examination question in economics touches upon the economic problem and its related concepts. For the most part, specific knowledge of the economic problem will be tested by objective-test questions rather than by data-response questions. You should expect up to two objective-test questions on the terms and concepts listed in this chapter: OTQ 1 in the Questions and Answers section of this Guide is a typical example.

Common examination errors

Commonly made mistakes on the economic problem include the following:
- Failure to appreciate that almost all problems and issues in economics involve the problem of scarcity and its related concepts.
- Failure to relate scarcity to the need for rationing, and to the role of rationing mechanisms such as the price mechanism and queues and waiting lists.
- Inaccurate drawing of production possibility diagrams.
- Not understanding the importance of the assumption of maximising behaviour in economic theory.
- Confusing positive and normative statements (see the examiner comment on OTQ 1 on p. 52 for an explanation of the difference).

- Economics is the study of economising.
- Economics answers questions on what to produce, how to produce and for whom to produce, in a world in which most of the resources are limited relative to wants and needs.
- Scarcity is the fundamental economic problem.
- A production possibility frontier shows the different combinations of goods that can be produced from available resources.
- Households and firms have economic objectives that they wish to maximise.

- Free goods are available at zero price because they are not scarce and because no costs of production are involved.
- The production of economic goods uses up scarce resources and people have to economise in their use.
- A normative statement involves a value judgement whereas a positive statement can be tested to see if it is true or false.

Supply and demand in competitive markets

These notes relate to AQA specification section 3.1.2 and prepare you to answer examination questions on the following:
- how the price mechanism establishes an equilibrium within a market
- how the market adjusts to a new equilibrium following a shift of demand or supply

Knowledge check 3

What is meant by equilibrium in economics?

Essential information

What is a market?

A **market**, which is a meeting of buyers and sellers for the purpose of exchanging goods or services, exists in the **market sector** of the economy. Figure 2 illustrates the key features of a market.

Demand and supply curves in a market

The **demand curve** shows the quantities of a good that households or consumers *plan* to purchase at different prices, and the **supply curve** shows how much firms or producers *plan* to supply at different prices. At all prices (except the **equilibrium price**) it is impossible for both households and firms simultaneously to fulfil their market plans. For example, at price P_1 firms would like to supply Q_2, but households are only willing to purchase Q_1. **Planned supply** is greater than **planned demand**, resulting in an **excess supply**. By contrast, at price P_2 households wish to buy Q_4 but firms restrict supply to Q_3, and **excess demand** results. At any price other than P^*, which is the equilibrium price, there will be either excess supply or excess demand, with either the firms or the households unable to fulfil their market plans. The market is in **disequilibrium** when there is excess supply or excess demand.

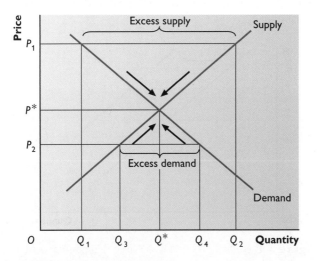

Figure 2 The price mechanism operating within a market

How an equilibrium price is achieved

In economics, we assume that firms respond to excess supply by reducing the price they are prepared to accept, while conversely households bid up the price to eliminate excess demand. The price falls or rises until equilibrium is achieved. The **equilibrium price** is the only price that satisfies both households and firms, which consequently have no reason to change their market plans. At P^* planned demand = planned supply.

Shifts of demand or supply curves

Market equilibrium may be disturbed by a shift of either the demand curve or the supply curve. A demand curve will shift if any of the factors influencing demand, other than the good's own price, changes. These factors are called the conditions of demand.

The conditions of demand

The conditions of demand, factors that may cause the demand curve to shift to the left or to the right, include income, taxes imposed on income (income tax), welfare benefits given to people, tastes and preferences, the prices of **substitute goods** and the prices of **complementary goods** (or goods in joint demand).

For example, an increase in income shifts demand curves rightward — but only for normal goods. A normal good is defined as a good for which demand increases when income increases. By contrast, an inferior good is a good (such as poor-quality food) for which demand falls as income increases. If the good is inferior, an increase in income shifts the demand curve leftward. Figure 3 shows a rightward shift of demand from D_1 to D_2, caused perhaps by a fall in the price of a good in joint demand (a complementary good) or by a successful advertising campaign for the product. Before the shift of demand, P_1 was an equilibrium price. Following the shift of demand, this is no longer the case. Planned demand is greater than planned supply and there is

equilibrium price
the price that clears the market, at which there is no excess demand or excess supply.

Examiner tip
Usually you should start your answer to part [03] of a data-response question on a market by drawing a graph to show a market in equilibrium.

Knowledge check 4

Explain the difference between a shift of demand and an adjustment of demand.

substitute goods goods that are in competing demand such as Sony and Nintendo games consoles.

complementary goods goods that are in joint demand (they go together) such as cars and petrol.

excess demand of $Q_2 - Q_1$ in the market. To relieve the excess demand, the price rises to a new equilibrium at P_2.

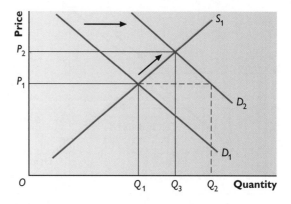

Figure 3 The effect of a rightward shift of demand in a market

The conditions of supply

By contrast, if **conditions of supply** change, the supply curve shifts. The conditions of supply include **costs of production**, **taxes levied upon firms** by government (**indirect taxes**) and **subsidies** given by the government to firms. For example, an increase in labour costs would shift the supply curve upward (or leftward).

Composite demand, derived demand and joint supply

You must take care not to confuse joint demand and competing demand with composite demand and derived demand. Composite demand is demand for a good which has more than one use: for example, barley can be used as an animal feed or to make beer. This example also illustrates derived demand, since the demand for barley is derived from the demand for beer and the demand for meat products. The demand for labour is also a derived demand, which increases when the demand for the goods they help to produce goes up. Finally, joint supply occurs when the production of one good affects the production of a byproduct produced from the same raw material. In some situations, increased supply of one good inevitably increases the supply of the byproduct: for example, the supply of cow hides inevitably increases when more cattle are slaughtered to meet the demand for meat. In other situations, production of one good is increased by reducing production of the byproduct: for example, increased demand for diesel fuel may cause oil companies to refine more diesel and less petrol from a barrel of oil.

Examination skills

The skills most likely to be tested by objective-test and data-response questions on supply and demand in competitive markets are as follows:

- Interpreting a graph or table to describe the changes taking place over a period of time in the price of a good.

Examiner tip

Part [03] of a data-response question on a market typically asks you to shift either the demand curve or the supply curve to a new position and a new equilibrium price.

Knowledge check 5

Give another example of a good which is in composite demand.

- Interpreting a graph or table to compare changes in the prices of two goods.
- Drawing a supply and demand diagram to illustrate the market in equilibrium.
- Identifying a change in either the conditions of demand or the conditions of supply, and the resulting shift of either the demand curve or the supply curve.
- Explaining how the market mechanism operates to eliminate excess demand or excess supply, and the adjustment of the market to a new equilibrium.
- Distinguishing between a shift of a demand or supply curve, and an adjustment in response to a price change along a demand or supply curve.
- Analysing goods in joint demand (complementary goods, such as cars and petrol), competing demand (substitute goods, such as tea and coffee) and joint supply (such as beef and leather).

Examination questions

You should expect about four or five objective-test questions on supply and demand in competitive markets. OTQ 2 in the Questions and Answers section of this Guide is a typical example. Supply and demand is also likely to figure prominently in at least one of the two optional data-response questions. The AQA specification states that 'students should be able to apply their knowledge of the basic model of demand and supply to markets, including commodity markets such as oil and copper markets, agriculture, healthcare, housing, sport and leisure'.

Markets for primary products are likely to figure prominently in data-response questions set on supply and demand in competitive markets. Expect the question to focus on a particular market, such as the copper market or the market for an agricultural commodity such as wheat or maize. Questions may also be set on industrial markets for manufactured goods, such as flat-screen TV sets or video games.

Common examination errors

Commonly made mistakes on supply and demand in competitive markets include the following:
- Confusing a shift of a demand curve with an adjustment along a demand curve (likewise, confusing a shift of a supply curve with an adjustment along a supply curve).
- Confusing the factors that cause a demand curve to shift with those that cause a supply curve to shift.
- Drawing supply and demand graphs with the curves and axes wrongly labelled.
- Confusing excess demand and excess supply.
- Confusing normal goods and inferior goods when a change in income causes a demand curve to shift.
- Confusing composite demand and derived demand with other demand concepts such as joint demand.

Summary

- A market is a meeting of buyers and sellers for the purpose of exchanging goods or services.
- Two of the main features of a market are a demand curve and a supply curve.
- Market equilibrium occurs when demand equals supply.
- Disequilibrium in a market means there is either excess demand or excess supply in the market.
- In a competitive market, the market mechanism (or price mechanism) causes the price to rise or fall to get rid of excess demand or excess supply.
- Market equilibrium may be disturbed by a shift in either the demand curve or the supply curve.

- A change in a condition of demand, such as consumers' incomes, causes the demand curve to shift to a new position.
- Likewise, a change in a condition of supply, such as costs of production, causes the supply curve to shift to a new position.
- Composite demand is demand for a good which has more than one use, while derived demand means that the demand for one good is derived from the demand for another good.
- Joint supply occurs when the production of one good affects the production of a byproduct produced from the same raw material.

Elasticity

These notes relate to AQA specification section 3.1.2 and prepare you to answer examination questions on the following:

- elasticities of demand and supply
- the application of appropriate elasticities to explain how particular markets function and to analyse problems of resource allocation in such markets

Essential information

The meaning of elasticity

Whenever a change in one variable (such as a good's price) causes a change to occur in a second variable (such as the quantity of the good that firms are prepared to supply), an elasticity can be calculated. Elasticity measures the proportionate response or change in a second variable following an initial change in a first variable. For example, if a 5% increase in price were to cause firms to increase supply more than proportionately (say, by 10%), supply would be **elastic**. If the response were less than proportionate (for example, an increase in supply of only 3%), supply would be **inelastic**. And if the change in price were to induce an exactly proportionate change in supply, supply would be neither elastic nor inelastic — this is called **unit elasticity of supply**.

Elasticity formulae

The formulae for the four elasticities you need to know are:

(1) Price elasticity of demand $= \dfrac{\text{proportionate change in quantity demanded}}{\text{proportionate change in price}}$

(2) Income elasticity of demand $= \dfrac{\text{proportionate change in quantity demanded}}{\text{proportionate change in income}}$

(3) Cross elasticity of demand for good A with respect to the price of B $= \dfrac{\text{proportionate change in quantity of A demanded}}{\text{proportionate change in price of B}}$

(4) Price elasticity of supply $= \dfrac{\text{proportionate change in quantity supplied}}{\text{proportionate change in price}}$

Price elasticity of demand

Price elasticity of demand measures consumers' responsiveness to a change in a good's own price. The factors which influence price elasticity of demand are:

- **Substitutability:** this is the most important determinant of price elasticity of demand. When a substitute exists for a product, consumers can respond to a price rise by switching expenditure away from the good, buying instead the substitute whose price has not risen. Demand for necessities tends to be inelastic as they have few substitutes. A substitute good is a good that can be used instead of another good: for example, apples as a substitute for pears.
- **Percentage of income:** goods or services upon which households spend a large proportion of their income tend to be in more elastic demand than small items upon which only a fraction of income is spent.
- **The 'width' of the market definition:** the demand for Shell petrol is much more price elastic than the market demand for petrol produced by all the oil companies.
- **Time:** although there are exceptions, demand for many goods and services is more elastic in the long run than in the short run because it takes time to respond to a price change.

Knowledge check 6

Why is the demand for Tesco's salt more price elastic than the demand for salt as a generic product?

Income elasticity of demand

Income elasticity of demand — which measures how demand responds to a change in income — is always negative for an inferior good and positive for a normal good. The quantity demanded of an inferior good falls as income rises, whereas demand for a normal good rises with income. Normal goods are sometimes further subdivided into superior goods or luxuries, for which the income elasticity of demand is greater than unity, and basic goods, with an income elasticity of less than 1.

Knowledge check 7

The income elasticity of demand for a good is +2.3. What does this statistic tell us about the good?

Cross elasticity of demand

Cross elasticity of demand measures the responsiveness of demand for one commodity to changes in the price of another good. The cross elasticity of demand between two goods or services indicates the nature of the demand relationship between the goods. There are three possibilities: joint demand (negative cross elasticity); competing demand or substitutes (positive cross elasticity); and an absence of any discernible demand relationship (zero cross elasticity).

Knowledge check 8

The cross elasticity of demand for a good A with respect to the price of good B is −0.8. What does this statistic tell us about good A?

Price elasticity of supply

Price elasticity of supply measures the extent to which firms are prepared to increase output in response to a change in price. Its main determinants are as follows:

- **Length of the production period:** when firms convert raw materials into finished goods for sale in a production period of just a few hours or days, supply is more elastic than when several months are involved, as in many types of agricultural production.
- **Existence of spare capacity:** when a firm possesses spare capacity and when labour and raw materials are readily available, it is usually possible to increase production quickly in the short run.

- **Ease of accumulating stocks:** when unsold stocks of finished goods can be stored at low cost, firms will be able to meet any sudden increase in demand from stock. Supply also tends to be elastic when firms can quickly increase production by drawing on their stocks of raw materials.
- **Ease of factor substitution:** supply tends to be relatively elastic if firms can use different combinations of labour and capital to produce a particular level of output.
- **Number of firms in the market:** generally the greater the number of firms in the market, the more elastic is market or industry supply.
- **Time:** supply is completely inelastic in the market period or momentary period, often relatively inelastic in the short run, and much more elastic in the long run when a firm can change the scale of all its inputs or factors of production in response to a change in demand and price.

Indirect taxes, subsidies and price elasticity of demand

Imposing or raising an indirect tax shifts a good's supply curve upward, but the effect on price and the incidence of the tax (who bears the tax) depends on the elasticity of the demand curve. More generally, when a supply curve (or a demand curve) shifts, the extent to which price or quantity changes in the process of adjustment to the new equilibrium depends upon the elasticity of the other curve, i.e. the curve that does not shift. This very important point is illustrated in the three panels of Figure 4, which show a rightward shift of supply along demand curves of different elasticities.

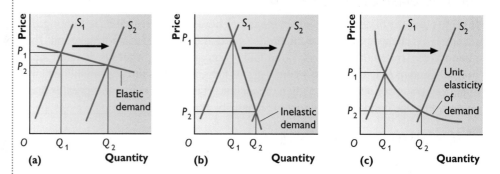

Figure 4 The extent to which price and quantity change following a shift of supply depends upon price elasticity of demand

Examiner tip
When you explain events occurring in a market, it is often relevant to discuss the price elasticity of either the demand curve and/or the supply curve.

When demand is elastic (Figure 4a), the quantity bought and sold adjusts much more than price. The reverse is true when demand is inelastic (Figure 4b). Finally, when demand is unit elastic (depicted in the rectangular hyperbola in Figure 4c), price and quantity change by equal percentages.

Examination skills

The skills most likely to be tested by objective-test and data-response questions on elasticity are as follows:
- Calculating an elasticity using the appropriate formula.
- Interpreting the economic meaning and significance of an elasticity.
- Drawing and explaining a diagram illustrating elastic or inelastic demand or supply.
- Explaining events in a market in terms of elasticities of demand and supply.

- Applying elasticity analysis to assess the economic effect of decisions made by firms or consumers.
- Evaluating the effects of government policies such as a decision to increase an indirect tax.

Examination questions

You should expect up to three multiple-choice questions on elasticity. OTQ 3 in the Questions and Answers section of this Guide is a typical example. The first part of a data-response question on a market may require a definition of one of the four elasticities, and the third part of the question may ask you to apply an elasticity concept to explain the effects of a shift of demand or supply.

Common examination errors

Commonly made mistakes on elasticity are:
- Confusing elasticity with slope. By definition, straight-line demand and supply curves have constant slopes, but elasticity varies from point to point along many (though not all) demand and supply curves.
- Missing out the word 'proportionate' or 'percentage' in elasticity formulae (as in 'proportionate change in quantity demanded').
- Incorrectly writing elasticity formulae 'upside down' (e.g. putting price on the top line and quantity on the bottom line of the formula for price elasticity of demand).
- Writing about the wrong elasticity — particularly about elasticity of *demand* when the question asks about elasticity of *supply*.
- Drifting into 'write all you know' mode, or churning out facts and diagrams for all the elasticities the student can think of, without applying knowledge selectively to address the issue posed by the question.

Summary

- Elasticity measures the *proportionate* response or change in a second variable following an initial change in a first variable.

- The four elasticities you need to know are price elasticity of demand, income elasticity of demand, cross elasticity of demand and price elasticity of supply.

- When demand is price elastic, a change in price leads to a *more than proportionate* change in demand. In this situation the price elasticity of demand is greater than 1 (or unity).

- When demand is price inelastic, a change in price leads to a *less than proportionate* change in demand. In this situation the price elasticity of demand is less than 1 (or unity).

- When price elasticity of demand equals 1 (or unity) a change in price leads to an *exactly proportionate* change in demand. In this situation the price elasticity of demand is neither elastic nor inelastic.

- Similar relationships hold for the other three elasticities.

- The existence of substitutes is the main determinant of price elasticity of demand.

- With income elasticity of demand, the plus or minus sign of the elasticity statistic tells us whether the good is a normal good or an inferior good.

- With cross elasticity of demand, the plus or minus sign of the elasticity statistic tells us whether the two goods are substitutes or complementary goods in joint demand.

- The existence or lack of spare capacity is one of the factors determining price elasticity of supply.

- When the supply curve of a good shifts — for example, when an indirect tax is imposed on the good — price elasticity of demand determines the extent to which the good's price changes.

Prices and resource allocation

These notes relate to AQA specification section 3.1.2 and prepare you to answer examination questions on:

- resource allocation in market economies and mixed economies
- the functions that prices perform when allocating scarce resources among competing uses in markets

Essential information

Prices in a market economy

Prices provide the main method through which scarce resources are allocated between competing uses in virtually all modern economies. In a pure **market economy** — made up solely of markets — the price mechanism is the only allocative mechanism solving the economic problem (apart from inheritance and other gifts, luck such as winning the lottery, and theft).

Prices in a mixed economy

However, most modern economies, including the UK economy, are not pure market economies. They are **mixed economies**, containing a mix of **private ownership** and **state ownership** of the means of production (capital), and a mix of market and non-market provision of goods and services, i.e. they have a **market sector** and a **non-market sector**. In the market sector, the price mechanism allocates scarce resources between competing uses. But in the non-market sector, the government uses the command mechanism or **planning mechanism** to provide goods and services such as police, roads and healthcare.

The three different types of economic system

Figure 5 illustrates three different types of economic system: **planned economies** (or **command economies**), **mixed economies** and **market economies**. The price mechanism operates within mixed and market economies, but only to a limited extent (for example, in black markets) in a largely planned economy (such as the communist economies of eastern Europe before the collapse of communism around 1990).

| Planned economies (command economies) The planning mechanism allocates scarce resources among competing uses | Mixed economies Mix of non-market and market, and public and private sectors | Market economies The price mechanism allocates scarce resources among competing uses in the markets that make up the economy |

Figure 5 Planned (command), mixed and market economies

Conditions necessary for a market to operate successfully

Within a market economy or the market sector of a mixed economy, three conditions are necessary for a market to operate successfully:

---

allocative mechanism An allocative mechanism, such as the price mechanism, is the mechanism through which scarce resources are allocated between competing uses.

Knowledge check 9

Distinguish between the market mechanism and the command mechanism.

economic system An economic system is set of institutions in which scarce resources are allocated between competing uses.

black market If conventional markets are prevented from working properly, a secondary market may come into existence to deal with, for example, the problem of excess demand or to provide a banned good. A secondary market is often called a black market.

- The individual buyers and sellers decide what, how, how much, where and when to trade or exchange.
- They do so with reference to their self-interest and to the alternatives or opportunities open to them; the exchange must be voluntary; if one party forces a transaction upon the other, it is not a market transaction.
- Prices convey information to buyers and sellers about self-interest and opportunities; for a market to allocate resources among different types of activity and to coordinate economic activity throughout the economy, prices must respond to the forces of supply and demand.

Three main functions of prices

Prices perform three main functions in a market or mixed economy:

- **The signalling function.** Prices signal what is available, conveying the information that allows all the traders in the market to plan and coordinate their economic activities. Markets will function inefficiently, sometimes breaking down completely, leading to market failure, if prices signal wrong or misleading information.
- **The incentive function.** Prices create incentives for economic agents (e.g. households and firms) to behave and make decisions in ways consistent with pursuing and achieving the fulfilment of their self-interest.
- **The allocative function or rationing function.** For markets to operate in an orderly and efficient manner, the buyers and sellers in the market must respond to the incentives provided by the price mechanism. Suppose that, in a particular market, demand increases relative to supply, causing the market price to rise. An immediate result is that the rising price limits to some extent the increase in the demand for the good or service, which has now become more expensive compared to other goods, thereby creating for consumers an incentive to economise in its use. However, simultaneously, the possibility of higher profits creates for firms an incentive to shift resources into producing the goods and services whose relative price has risen and to demand more resources, such as labour and capital, in order to increase production. In turn, this may bid up wages and the price of capital, creating for households and the owners of capital an incentive to switch the supply of labour and capital into industries where the prices of inputs or factors of production are rising. In this way, the changing prices of goods and services relative to each other allocate and ration the economy's scarce resources to the consumers and firms who are willing and able to pay most for them.

The invisible hand of the market

Over 200 years ago, the economist Adam Smith described how the **invisible** or **hidden hand of the market**, operating in competitive markets and through the pursuit of self-interest, achieves an allocation of resources that is also in society's interest. This remains the central view of all free-market economists, i.e. those who believe in the virtues of a competitive market economy subject to minimum government intervention. However, when the invisible hand fails to work in the manner just described, **market failure** and **resource misallocation** occur (see pp. 28–32).

Examination skills

The skills most likely to be tested by multiple-choice or data-response questions on prices and resource allocation are as follows:

Examiner tip
It is important to recognise that when markets perform well, prices convey accurate information and create suitable incentives to which economic agents can respond. But when one or more of the three functions of prices performs unsatisfactorily, or in extreme cases breaks down completely, market failure occurs

Knowledge check 10
How does the price mechanism operate in labour markets?

free-market economists those who believe that resource allocation should be left solely or mostly to the market mechanism (or price mechanism) and to private enterprise or free enterprise.

- Identifying and explaining the signalling, incentive creating, and allocative functions of prices.
- Applying knowledge of the functions of prices to a particular market, such as an agricultural market.
- Explaining how the price mechanism functions within a market to eliminate excess supply or demand and achieve equilibrium.
- Explaining how the price mechanism allocates resources among markets as consumers substitute cheaper for more expensive goods, and firms move from less profitable into more profitable markets.
- Evaluating how well or how badly prices perform these functions.

Examination questions

You should expect one objective-test question that relates explicitly to the functions of prices. OTQ 4 in the Questions and Answers section of this Guide is a typical example. Data-response questions might also require application of your knowledge and understanding of the functions of prices. Even if a data-response question does not ask explicitly about the signalling, incentive and allocative functions of prices, relevant application of knowledge of these functions can often earn high marks. This is particularly true of the last part of data-response questions, for which a levels of response marking scheme is used to allocate the 25 marks available. Although a question makes no explicit mention of the function of prices, a good answer may require application of these concepts.

Appropriate application of knowledge of the functions of prices in the task of resource allocation in the economy may well be the key skill that raises the standard of your answer from Level 3 to Level 4 or 5.

Common examination errors

Commonly made mistakes on prices and resource allocation are:
- A failure to understand the decentralised and unorganised nature of a market.
- An inability to relate the functions of prices to the economic problem of scarcity.
- A failure to relate the functions of prices to the pursuit of self-interest, to consumers' utility-maximising objectives and to firms' profit-maximising objectives.
- A lack of appreciation that 'market failure' and resource misallocation occur when prices malfunction.

Summary

- Prices provide the main method through which scarce resources are allocated between competing uses in virtually all modern economies.
- In the market sector of a mixed economy, the price mechanism allocates scarce resources between competing uses. But in the non-market sector, the government uses the command mechanism or planning mechanism to provide and allocate goods and services.
- For a market to allocate resources among different types of activity and to coordinate economic activity throughout the economy, prices must respond to the forces of supply and demand.
- The three main functions that prices perform in markets are signalling, creating incentives and rationing or allocating scarce resources between competing uses.
- The metaphor of the invisible hand of the market is often used to convey the way prices allocate scarce resources between competing uses.

Production and efficiency

These notes relate to AQA specification section 3.1.3 and prepare you to answer examination questions on the following:
- the meaning of production and productivity
- key concepts relating to production: specialisation and the division of labour; economies of scale and diseconomies of scale
- the nature of productive efficiency

Essential information

Production and the factors of production

Production is simply the process by which inputs are converted into outputs. The inputs into the production process are the four **factors of production** listed in Figure 6: namely, land, labour, capital and the entrepreneurial input, often called enterprise. The eventual outputs are the consumer goods and services that go to make up our standard of living, though inputs are of course also used to produce the capital goods that are necessary for eventual production of consumer goods.

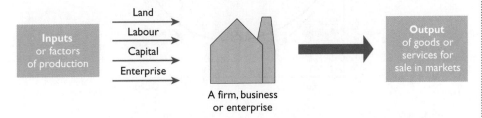

Figure 6 A firm undertaking production

The entrepreneur ultimately decides what, where, how and how much to produce, and also how much of the other factor services to employ. The entrepreneur is the decision maker and financial risk taker in a business. In recent years, television programmes such as *The Apprentice* and *Dragons' Den* have brought entrepreneurs to the attention of the general public.

Production and a firm's main business objective

Economists assume that the entrepreneur (and the firm) has a **profit-maximising objective**. Profit is the difference between the total sales **revenue** earned from the sale of the goods or services produced by the firm, and the total **costs of production** incurred when paying the factors of production for their services. Profit is thus the entrepreneur's reward for decision-making and financial risk-taking.

Productivity

If we assume that the capital and land employed by a firm are fixed and cannot be altered, at least in the short run, the only way a firm can increase production is by employing more factors of production such as labour. To start with, as more

consumer good also known as a final good — literally a good or service bought by consumers. Examples include a meal consumed by a family in a restaurant and consumer durable goods such as a household television set.

capital good also known as an intermediate good and an investment good — a good used by a firm to produce other goods. An example is a robot used in car production.

profit total sales revenue minus total production costs.

labour productivity
output per worker, not to be confused with capital productivity, which is output per unit of capital.

Examiner tip
Productivity and production possibility frontiers (see p. 11) are just as important when you study Unit 2: The National Economy.

economies of scale
falls in average costs of production as the size or scale of a firm increases.

workers are employed, labour productivity may rise, as the workers benefit from **specialisation** and the **division of labour**, i.e. different workers specialising in different tasks. In the economy as a whole, different firms and industries also specialise in producing different goods and services. This, of course, necessitates **trade** and **exchange**, which take place in the economy's markets.

Economies and diseconomies of scale

Labour productivity also rises when a firm benefits from economies of scale (but falls if it eventually suffers from diseconomies of scale). Economies and diseconomies of scale are illustrated in Figure 7, which shows how a firm's average costs of production may change as it increases the size or scale of its operations.

Economies of scale occur when a firm experiences falling average costs as it increases its size and scale and produces more output. If a firm increases beyond a certain size (point X in Figure 7), average costs begin to rise and diseconomies of scale set in.

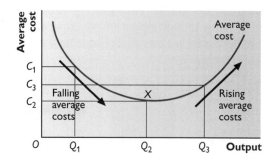

Figure 7 A firm's average cost curve and economies and diseconomies of scale

There are various types of economy of scale, such as technical and managerial economies. An example of a **technical economy of scale** is a **volume economy**. When a warehouse is doubled in dimension, its storage capacity actually increases eightfold. As a result, average storage costs fall as the size or scale of storage capacity increases.

diseconomies of scale
increases in average costs of production as the size or scale of a firm increases.

Knowledge check 12
Name one other type of economy of scale besides those mentioned here.

However, diseconomies of scale could also set in as storage capacity increases. Stored materials may become mislaid or lost more easily, and the firm owning the warehouse may be tempted to store unnecessary stocks of raw materials or goods awaiting sale. **Managerial economies of scale** occur because large firms can employ specialist and more highly skilled managers. On the other hand, too many managers and a breakdown of communication between them result in managerial diseconomies of scale.

Productive efficiency

The level of output produced at the lowest average cost of production is known as the productively efficient level of output. When economies of scale are possible, expanding the size or scale of the firm can get rid of productive inefficiency and move output towards the productively efficient level. Productive efficiency is shown at point X in Figure 7, when economies of scale have been benefited from to the full, but before diseconomies of scale set in. In this situation, the firm's average cost curve is 'U-shaped', and productive efficiency occurs at the lowest point on the 'U'.

Examination skills

The skills most likely to be tested by objective-test and data-response questions on production and efficiency are:
- Defining and explaining the meaning of production, specialisation, division of labour, economies of scale and productive efficiency.
- Discussing the reasons for the growth of a firm, or the advantages resulting from growth.
- Relating specialisation and the division of labour to the role of markets in the economy.
- Relating over-specialisation and diseconomies of scale to possible causes of market failure.
- Analysing monopoly in terms of economies of scale.

Examination questions

You should expect up to three objective-test questions on production, efficiency, specialisation, the division of labour and economies and diseconomies of scale. OTQ 5 in the Questions and Answers section of this Guide is a typical example. DRQs 5 and 6 illustrate ways in which knowledge and understanding of the key concepts in this section of the specification may be tested in a data-response question. The scenario in DRQ 3 centres on labour productivity and economies of scale in the car industry, and also in the transport of freight in containers by ship and by rail. Market-based questions such as DRQ 1 could well ask for a discussion of whether the market functions efficiently. Practise the skill of assessing whether the market depicted in a data-response question is productively efficient.

Common examination errors

Commonly made mistakes on production and efficiency are:
- Confusing production and productivity.
- Not relating economies of scale to a 'U'-shaped average cost curve.
- Failure to appreciate how markets facilitate specialisation and the division of labour.
- Writing over-long descriptive accounts of types of economy of scale.
- Confusing economies and diseconomies of scale.
- Failure to understand, correctly apply and illustrate the concept of productive efficiency.

- Production is the process or set of processes through which inputs are converted into outputs.
- The inputs into production are called factors of production.
- Land, labour, capital and enterprise, or the entrepreneurial input, are the four factors of production.
- Profit is the entrepreneur's reward for decision-making and financial risk-taking.
- Production should not be confused with productivity.
- Labour productivity is output per worker.

- Specialisation and the division of labour can increase labour productivity.
- Specialisation and the division of labour also lead to trade and exchange.
- Labour productivity rises when a firm benefits from economies of scale but falls if the firm suffers from diseconomies of scale.
- Economies of scale are falling average costs of production when the size or scale of the firm increases.
- Productive efficiency occurs when average costs of production are at their lowest level.

Market failure, public goods and externalities

These notes relate to AQA specification section 3.1.4 and prepare you to answer examination questions on:

- the meaning of market failure
- the failure of markets to provide public goods
- the tendency of a market to over-provide or under-provide a good when externalities are discharged in the course of the good's production or consumption

Essential information

The meaning of market failure

market failure can also be defined as a market functioning inefficiently or a market functioning inequitably, or as a situation in which one or more of the three functions of prices breaks down.

private goods goods such as apples, which are both excludable and rival.

Market failure occurs whenever a market, or the complete absence of a market, leads to a misallocation of resources. With some market failures, markets do exist, but they function badly. For example, markets produce too little of a merit good such as healthcare, and too much of a demerit good such as tobacco or crack cocaine.

Private goods

Most goods are private goods, possessing two important characteristics. The owners can exercise private property rights, preventing other people from using a good or consuming its benefits — unless they are prepared to pay a price for the good in the market. This property is called **excludability**. The second characteristic possessed by a private good is **rivalry** or **diminishability**: when one person consumes the good, fewer of the benefits are available for other people.

Public goods

A public good exhibits the opposite characteristics of **non-excludability** and **non-rivalry** or **non-diminishability**. It is these that lead to market failure.

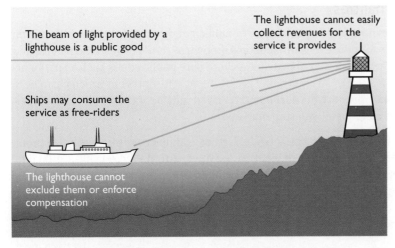

The beam of light provided by a lighthouse is a public good

The lighthouse cannot easily collect revenues for the service it provides

Ships may consume the service as free-riders

The lighthouse cannot exclude them or enforce compensation

Figure 8 A lighthouse as a public good

Suppose an entrepreneur builds the lighthouse shown in Figure 8, and then tries to charge each ship benefiting from the service provided: namely, the beam of light. Providing ships pay up, the service can be provided commercially through the market. However, the market is likely to fail because the incentive function of prices breaks down (see p. 23). Because it is impossible to exclude free-riders (ships that benefit without paying), it may be impossible to collect enough revenue to cover costs. If too many ships decide to 'free-ride', profits cannot be made and the incentive to provide the service through the market disappears. The market thus fails to provide a service for which there is an obvious need; hence the case for alternative provision by the government in its public spending programme, or possibly by a charity.

Pure and non-pure public goods

You should distinguish between pure and non-pure public goods. National defence and police are examples of pure public goods — defined as public goods for which it is impossible to exclude free-riders. However, most public goods (street lighting, roads and lighthouses) are non-pure public goods. Methods can be devised for converting the goods into private goods by excluding free-riders (for example, electronic pricing of road use). Non-pure public goods can be provided by markets, although the second property of non-rivalry or non-diminishability means there is a case for providing all public goods free in order to encourage as much consumption as possible.

Missing markets

A pure public good provides an example of market failure resulting from the complete absence of a market. This is known as the problem of **missing markets**. With a pure public good, such as national defence, the market may just not exist. Assuming there is a need for public goods, some mechanism other than the market mechanism must be used to provide the goods. The usual response is for governments to provide public goods free at the point of use for consumers, with provision paid for collectively through taxation. Another possibility is provision by charities.

Knowledge check 13

Give an example of a person 'free-riding' on another person.

Examiner tip

You must not confuse a public good with a government good, which is any good provided by government.

pure public good a good such as a terrestrially broadcast television programme, that is both non-excludable and non-rival.

Knowledge check 14

Give an example, other than the ones listed here, of a market providing a non-pure public good.

Examiner tip

Remember that both public goods and externalities provide examples of missing markets.

Externalities

externality a public good, in the case of an **external benefit**, or a public 'bad', in the case of an **external cost**, that is 'dumped' on third parties 'outside the market'.

An **externality** is a special type of public good or public 'bad' which is 'dumped' by those who produce it on other people (known as third parties) who receive or consume it, whether or not they choose to. As with pure public goods such as national defence, the key feature of an externality is that there is no market in which it can be bought or sold. Since they are produced and received outside the market, externalities provide another example of 'missing markets'.

In addition, externalities provide further examples of the free-rider problem. The provider of an external benefit (or positive externality), such as a beautiful view, cannot charge a market price to any willing free-riders who enjoy it, while conversely, the unwilling free-riders who receive or consume external costs (or negative externalities), such as pollution and noise, cannot charge a price to the polluter for the 'bad' they reluctantly receive.

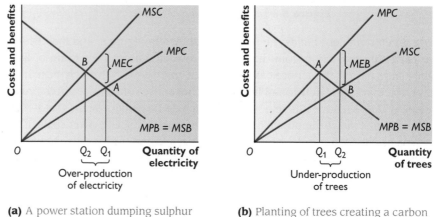

(a) A power station dumping sulphur dioxide in the atmosphere

(b) Planting of trees creating a carbon 'sink' which soaks up carbon dioxide

Figure 9 How externalities result in market failure

Examiner tip

With the use of diagrams such as those in Figure 9, you must be able to explain why externalities result in resource misallocation and market failure. This means you must understand the difference between private, external and social costs and benefits of production and consumption, and also the meaning of 'margin'.

Panel (a) of Figure 9 illustrates a **pure production externality**, generated in the course of production by a power station and received, for example, in the form of higher production costs by commercial fisheries. The privately optimal level of electricity generation (for the power station company) is shown at point A. To achieve the socially optimal level of production there is a case for levying a **pollution tax** on the power station company.

Analysing market failure using the concept of the margin

Whichever economic activity we are investigating, the 'marginal unit' is always the last unit of the activity undertaken. If one more unit of the activity is now added, the previous unit, which up to that point had been the marginal unit, can no longer be classified in this way. **Marginal cost** is the cost of producing the last unit of a good. This divides into **marginal private cost**, which is the extra cost incurred by the good's producer, and **marginal external** cost, which is the cost of the negative externalities 'spun-off' and dumped on third parties. The **marginal social cost** of production is the true marginal cost: namely, marginal private cost plus marginal external cost:

$$MSC = MPC + MEC$$

Turning to positive externalities, and using similar reasoning, we arrive at:

$$MSB = MPB + MEB$$

Consider the power station illustrated in panel (a) of Figure 9, which discharges pollution into the atmosphere in the course of producing electricity. We can view a negative production externality such as pollution as being that part of the true or real costs of production which the power station evades by dumping the 'bad' on others. The price that the consumer pays for the good (electricity) reflects only the money costs of production (the private cost), and not all the real costs, which include the external costs. In a market situation, the power station's output of electricity is thus under-priced. The incentive function of prices has broken down. Under-pricing encourages too much consumption of electricity, and therefore over-production of both electricity and the spin-off, pollution.

Panel (b) of Figure 9 illustrates the costs incurred and the benefits generated when a commercial forestry company plants trees. Tree planting produces a number of positive externalities or external benefits. These include improved water retention in the soil, and a 'carbon sink' effect, whereby trees absorb greenhouse or global-warming gases from the atmosphere. As a result, the **marginal social benefit** of tree-growing is greater than the **marginal private benefit** accruing to the forestry company. To maximise private benefit, the commercial forestry plants Q_1 trees (where $MPB = MPC$), but the socially optimal number of trees is greater, being Q_2 where $MSC = MSB$. If tree planting is left solely to market forces, the market fails because too few trees are planted. There is a case for the government granting a subsidy to the forestry companies to encourage them to plant more trees. (Now read the later section of this Guide on Government intervention in the market, pp. 42–45.)

Because the positive externality is generated in the course of production but received in consumption, panel (b) shows the MSC incurred by the whole community lying below the MPC to the power station company. The MEB enjoyed by the whole community is shown by the distance between the MPC and MSC curves. As is the case in panel (a), the privately optimal level of production (in this case tree planting) is shown at point A. However, the socially optimal number of new trees is higher and shown at point B.

Examination skills

The skills most likely to be tested by objective-test and data-response questions on public goods and externalities are:

- Explaining the meaning of market failure.
- Identifying examples of public goods and externalities.
- Explaining the reasons why market failure occurs in the case of public goods and externalities.
- Understanding the meaning of non-excludability and non-rivalry.

Knowledge check 15

What is the difference between marginal cost and average cost?

Examiner tip

Candidates often fail to understand that externalities are generated and received outside the market. Make sure you can give examples of external costs and external benefits and are aware of the difference between production and consumption externalities.

Examiner tip

You might be puzzled by the label MEB in Figure 9(b). Planting trees creates external benefits for society as a whole. However, a **positive** benefit can be viewed as a **negative** cost. Hence, MEB is a negative MEC.

- Relating the market failure to the breakdown of the incentive function of prices.
- Using diagrams to explain why market failure occurs when externalities are generated.
- Explaining how externalities are produced and consumed 'outside the market'.
- Assessing the case for government intervention to correct the market failure.

Examination questions

You should expect up to three or four objective-test questions on public goods and externalities. OTQ 6 in the Questions and Answers section of this Guide is a typical example. Part [03] of DRQ 4 also tests knowledge of externalities and of government policies that might reduce or eliminate negative externalities. Along with merit goods and private goods, knowledge of public goods is tested in DRQ 6.

Common examination errors

Commonly made mistakes on public goods and externalities are:

- Confusing a public good, such as defence, with a merit good, such as healthcare (see p. 33).
- Wrongly defining a public good as a good provided by the government.
- Confusing a public good with a free good.
- Failing to explain how and why the market fails in the case of public goods and externalities.
- Not understanding that markets can and do provide public goods, providing methods are devised for excluding free-riders.
- Naively arguing that government intervention always succeeds in correcting market failure.

Summary

- Market failure occurs whenever a market or the lack of a market leads to resource misallocation.
- Private goods are excludable and rival.
- Public goods are non-excludable and non-rival.
- A free-rider can consume or benefit from a good without paying for the good.
- Public goods divide into pure and non-pure public goods.
- A missing market occurs when a market completely collapses and fails to function at all.
- A key feature of an externality is that there is no market in which it can be traded.

- Externalities divide into external benefits (or positive externalities) and external costs (or negative externalities).
- Externalities also divide into production externalities and consumption externalities.
- The 'marginal unit' is always the *last* unit of an activity being undertaken.
- Marginal cost is the cost of producing the last unit of a good.
- Marginal social cost is marginal private cost plus marginal external cost
- Likewise, marginal social benefit is marginal private benefit plus marginal external benefit.

Merit and demerit goods, income and wealth inequalities, and labour immobility

These notes relate to AQA specification section 3.1.4 and prepare you to answer examination questions on:

- under-consumption of merit goods
- over-consumption of demerit goods
- inequalities in the distributions of income and wealth
- labour immobility as a cause of market failure

Essential information

Merit goods

A **merit good**, such as education or healthcare, is a good or service for which the social benefits of consumption enjoyed by the whole community exceed the private benefits received by the consumer. Consumption by an individual produces positive externalities that benefit the wider community.

Whereas markets may fail to provide any quantity at all of a pure public good, such as defence, they can certainly provide education and healthcare, as the existence of private fee-paying schools and hospitals clearly demonstrates. However, if schools and hospitals are available *only* through the market at prices unadjusted by subsidy, people (especially the poor) will choose to consume too little of their services. The resulting under-consumption of merit goods represents a misallocation of resources.

Demerit goods

As their name suggests, **demerit goods** are the opposite of merit goods. The social costs to the whole community which result from the consumption of a demerit good, such as tobacco or alcohol, exceed the private costs incurred by the consumer. This is because consumption by an individual produces negative externalities that harm the wider community. The private cost can be measured by the money cost of purchasing the good, together with any health damage suffered by the person consuming the good. But the social costs of consumption also include the cost of the negative externalities: for example, the costs of damage and injury inflicted on other people, resulting from tobacco smoke, and road accidents caused by drunken drivers. Thus, if demerit goods are provided only through the market, at prices unadjusted by taxation, people will choose to consume too much of the goods. Again, the resulting over-consumption of demerit goods results in resource misallocation.

merit good a good or service such as education, for which the social benefits of consumption exceed the private benefits.

Knowledge check 16

Distinguish between a merit good and a public good.

Examiner tip

Many exam students assert that any good that is 'good for you' is a merit good, and that any good that is 'bad for you' is a demerit good. These assertions are wrong.

demerit good a good or service such as cocaine for which the social costs of consumption exceed the private costs.

Merit goods and the information problem

Merit goods and demerit goods can possess a further characteristic (besides the divergence between private and social costs and benefits) which leads to their under-consumption or over-consumption. Individuals consuming merit and demerit goods may not act in their own best interest because they consider only *short-term* utility maximisation rather than *long-term* utility maximisation. For the individual concerned, the **long-term private benefits** of consuming a merit good, such as education and healthcare, exceed the **short-term private benefits**. For example, in a market situation, many people under-purchase healthcare services such as regular dental checks, and end up suffering the consequences later in life. People are likely to choose too little of the merit good early in life, and later in life they may wish they had consumed more. This is an example of an information problem.

Demerit goods and the information problem

Similarly, with a demerit good such as tobacco, the **long-term private costs** of consumption can exceed the **short-term private costs**. A teenage boy or girl who develops a smoking habit may regret later in life the decision to start smoking, particularly if he or she eventually contracts a smoking-related disease. With both merit and demerit goods, many economists argue that an authority outside the individual, such as the state, is a better judge than individuals themselves of what is good for them. The state should thus encourage the consumption of merit goods and discourage the consumption of demerit goods for the individual's own interest, as well as for the wider social interest.

Examples of merit goods and demerit goods

The goods listed in the left-hand panel of Table 1 are generally regarded as merit goods, while those in the right-hand panel are considered to be demerit goods. However, for the 'goods' listed in the middle panel, such as contraception, the position is less clear-cut. Because people have different values and ethics (often related to their religions), contraception is viewed by some people as a merit good, but by others as a demerit good. Whether a good is classified as a merit good or a demerit good, or indeed as neither, thus depends crucially on the value judgements of the person making the classification. This provides an important example of the distinction between positive and normative statements (see pp. 12–13).

Table 1 Classifying merit and demerit goods

Merit Goods	Merit or Demerit Goods?	Demerit Goods
Education	Contraception	Tobacco
Healthcare, e.g. vaccination, dental care, AIDS testing	Abortion	Heroin and other hard drugs
Crash helmets	Sterilisation	Alcohol
Car seat belts		Pornography
Museums		Prostitution

---

information problem occurs when people make wrong decisions because they don't possess or they ignore relevant information.

Knowledge check 17

Is there a case for the state not intervening in the provision of merit and demerit goods?

Examiner tip

In an exam answer, you can define a merit or a demerit good either in terms of the externalities generated when the good is consumed, or in terms of the information problem associated with the consumption of the good.

positive statement a statement of fact, or one that can be scientifically tested to see if it is true or false.

normative statement a statement of opinion based on value judgement

Diagrams illustrating merit goods and demerit goods

Figure 10 includes two diagrams illustrating how, if demerit goods and merit goods are available in markets at prices respectively unadjusted by taxation or subsidy, too much of the demerit good and too little of the merit good are produced and consumed.

On first sight, panels (a) and (b) in Figure 10 seem to be similar to the two diagrams in Figure 9 (see p. 30). However, there are subtle differences between the two pairs of diagrams. Figure 9 shows the production of two goods (electricity and tree planting), which are not themselves deemed to be demerit or merit goods. By contrast, the two goods shown in Figure 10 are generally regarded to be a demerit good (tobacco) and a merit good (healthcare) by most people living in high-income, developed countries such as the UK.

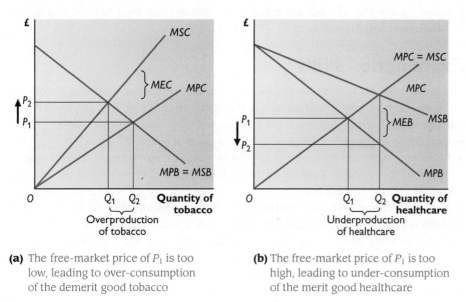

Examiner tip

Think how you could redraw Figure 10(b) to be similar to Figure 9(b). The subsidised price of healthcare would be determined at point B on your redrawn diagram.

(a) The free-market price of P_1 is too low, leading to over-consumption of the demerit good tobacco

(b) The free-market price of P_1 is too high, leading to under-consumption of the merit good healthcare

Figure 10 Demerit and merit goods and market failure

In both diagrams the price would be P_1 if the demerit or merit good were provided at a free-market price. However, this price is too low in the case of a demerit good, encouraging too much consumption, and too high in the case of a merit good, discouraging consumption. To achieve the socially optimal level of consumption (shown at Q_2 in both diagrams), the price of tobacco must be raised (for example, through taxation), and the price of healthcare cut (for example, through subsidy). In both diagrams, price P_2 achieves the socially optimal outcome.

Inequalities in the distribution of income and wealth

Economists have different views on whether inequalities in the distributions of income and wealth should be regarded as market failures. While there is general agreement that a completely unregulated market economy produces significant inequalities, some economists believe that government intervention to redistribute income and wealth destroys incentives that are vital for a market economy to function

income a *flow* concept, measured for example as money received per period of time, e.g. per week or per month.

wealth a *stock* concept, namely the value now of assets, including money, accumulated over time.

Knowledge check 18

What is the difference between equality and equity?

immobility of labour the inability of labour to move from one job to another, either for occupational reasons, e.g. the need for training, or for geographical reasons, e.g. the cost of moving to another part of the country.

efficiently. In their view, such intervention leads to worse problems of **government failure** (see p. 44).

Immobility of labour

Usually when economists talk of market failure, they refer to failures occurring in a **goods market** or market for products, such as over-production of demerit goods. However, market failure can also occur in labour markets, through the immobility of labour. Occupational and geographical immobility of labour mean that economic resources are not fully utilised in areas of high unemployment, while at the same time economic growth is held back by labour shortages in areas, regions and countries benefiting from full employment. According to free market theory, the problem can be cured through wage rates rising in areas of labour shortage, such as London and the southeast, and falling in areas of labour surplus, such as Northern Ireland. However, in practice, the market mechanism fails to solve the problem, and labour shortages and surpluses persist.

Examination skills

The skills most likely to be tested by objective-test or data-response questions on merit and demerit goods, inequalities in the distributions of income and wealth, and labour immobility are:

- Explaining why a particular good is a merit good or a demerit good.
- Explaining why markets under-supply merit goods and over-supply demerit goods.
- Applying the concept of equity to the analysis of the distributions of income and wealth.
- Distinguishing between the distributions of income and wealth.
- Using cost and benefit diagrams to analyse merit and demerit goods.
- Identifying appropriate government policies for correcting the market failures associated with merit and demerit goods, the distributions of income and wealth, and labour immobility (see pp. 42–45).
- Evaluating the extent to which these policies succeed in correcting the market failure.

Examination questions

You should expect up to three or four objective-test questions on merit and demerit goods, and inequalities in the distributions of income and wealth. OTQ 7 in the Questions and Answers section of this Guide is a typical example. These market failures may feature in one of the two optional data-response questions. See DRQs 5 and 6 for examples. An alleged demerit good (lads' mags) provides the scenario for DRQ 5, whereas the data in DRQ 6 centre on education as a merit good. Both questions test knowledge and understanding of how governments intervene in markets to try to correct market failures (see pp. 42–45) as well as the reasons why markets fail to provide the socially optimal quantity of merit and demerit goods (which is covered by these revision notes).

Common examination errors

Commonly made mistakes on merit and demerit goods, inequalities in the distributions of income and wealth, and labour immobility are:

- Wrongly classifying merit goods such as healthcare and education as public goods because they are often provided by the state in its public spending programme.
- Stating that merit goods are not private goods.
- Confusing a demerit good with an economic 'bad' — whereas a 'good' yields utility when consumed, a 'bad' such as pollution yields the opposite, namely disutility.
- Defining merit and demerit goods too loosely as 'any good that is good for you' in the case of a merit good, and as 'any good that is bad for you if over-consumed' in the case of a demerit good.
- Failing to understand that markets can produce merit and demerit goods, but they produce the 'wrong' quantity.
- Assuming that government intervention is always successful and corrects the market failure.
- Failing to recognise value judgements and the normative nature of these alleged market failures.
- Confusing wealth (a stock concept) with income (a flow concept).
- Not understanding the causes of labour immobility.

Summary

- A merit good is a good or service for which the social benefits of consumption enjoyed by the whole community exceed the private benefits received by the consumer.
- A demerit good is the opposite: namely, a good or service for which the social costs of consumption suffered by the whole community exceed the private costs the consumer suffers.
- Positive externalities are discharged when a merit good is consumed.
- Likewise, negative externalities are discharged when a demerit good is consumed.
- People consuming merit goods ignore or downplay information about the long-term private benefits that result from consumption. This factor contributes to under-consumption of merit goods.
- Likewise, people consuming demerit goods ignore or downplay information about the long-term private costs that result from consumption. This factor contributes to over-consumption of demerit goods.
- Economists have different views on whether inequalities in the distributions of income and wealth should be regarded as market failures.
- Immobility of labour also leads to market failure.

Monopolies and the allocation of resources

These notes relate to AQA specification section 3.1.4 and prepare you to answer examination questions on:

- the meaning of monopoly and monopoly power
- the causes of monopoly
- whether monopoly leads to resource misallocation or whether there may be circumstances in which the benefits of monopoly exceed the costs

Essential information

The meaning of monopoly

Economists use the word 'monopoly' in three rather different ways:

- **Pure monopoly** is a market structure in which there is only one firm. Because it is completely protected by barriers to entry, the firm faces no competition at all.
- Many firms, even those in quite competitive markets, possess a degree of monopoly power. Monopoly power (or market power) is the ability to influence the market: for example, by setting a price and using persuasive advertising to get consumers to buy the good. In pure monopoly, but also in highly concentrated markets (markets dominated by just a few firms), firms possess sufficient monopoly power to function as price makers rather than as price takers.
- Any industry dominated by a few large firms is often loosely called a monopoly, although more accurately it is an example of highly imperfect competition or oligopoly. (Oligopoly is an A2 rather than AS topic.)

The causes of monopoly

Monopoly power is strongest when a firm produces an essential good for which there are no substitutes — or when demand is relatively inelastic. Monopoly may be caused through:

- geographical reasons (e.g. a single grocery store in an isolated village)
- government creating monopolies that are protected from competition by the law (e.g. gambling casinos)
- control of market outlets and raw materials (e.g. breweries and oil companies denying competitors access to the pubs and petrol stations they own)
- using advertising as a barrier to entry: through saturation advertising, large firms can prevent small firms entering the market

Natural monopoly

Natural monopoly occurs when there is room in the market for only one firm benefiting from full economies of scale, which are falls in average costs of production resulting from an increase in the size or scale of a firm.

In the past, utility industries such as water, gas, electricity and the telephone industries were natural monopolies. The industries produced a service that was

pure monopoly a market or industry in which there is only one firm or producer.

delivered through a distribution network or grid of pipes or cables into millions of separate businesses and homes. Competition in the provision of distribution grids was regarded as wasteful, since it required the duplication of fixed capacity, therefore causing each supplier to incur unnecessarily high fixed costs. In recent years, technical progress, particularly in the telecommunications industry, has weakened and sometimes destroyed the natural monopoly status of the utility industries. Nevertheless, the UK government continues to regulate the utility industries to try to prevent the abuse of monopoly power.

Monopoly may lead to a misallocation of resources

Figure 11 illustrates how a monopoly may adversely affect **resource allocation**. In the absence of monopoly, a competitive industry produces output Q_1, which is sold at price P_1. If a monopoly is formed, the firm restricts output to Q_2 and raises the price to P_2, thereby exploiting consumers.

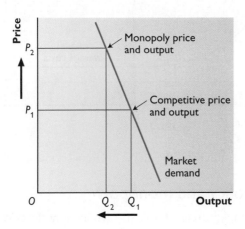

Figure 11 A monopoly restricting output and raising the price

Monopoly also leads to resource misallocation by:
- restricting consumer choice
- incurring higher costs of production than would be the case in a competitive market. This means the monopoly is **productively inefficient** (see pp. 26–27)
- exercising **producer sovereignty** at the expense of consumers. This means that unlike in a competitive market where **consumer sovereignty** rules, the monopoly fails to respond to consumers' wishes, preferring instead an 'easy life'. In effect, this means the 'producer is king' rather than the consumer.

The circumstances in which monopoly may improve resource allocation

Under certain circumstances, monopoly may be justified because it improves resource allocation. This can occur for two main reasons:

By achieving economies of scale, a monopoly can produce at lower average cost and be more productively efficient than smaller firms in a competitive industry. This is illustrated in Figure 12, which shows an industry in which there are economies of scale, but also a limited maximum size to the market. In such a situation there is

> **Knowledge check 20**
> Explain why the water industry is a natural monopoly.

> **resource allocation**
> how economic resources are allocated between different industries and eventually, as final goods, to different consumers.

> **Knowledge check 21**
> What is meant by a misallocation of resources?

only room in the market for one firm benefiting to the full from economies of scale: a natural monopoly.

A monopoly may use its monopoly power and monopoly profit to finance innovation in new products and better ways of making existing products. By contrast, if competitors can instantly copy any successful innovation, a competitive firm may lack the incentive to innovate, and in any case it may lack the profit needed to finance innovation. This argument is used to justify patent legislation, which gives firms an exclusive right to exploit their innovations for a number of years without being exposed to competition.

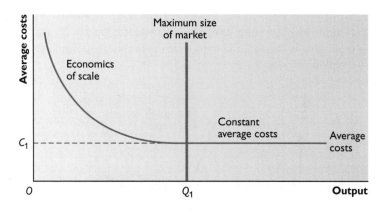

Figure 12 Monopoly occurs when there is room in the market for only one firm benefiting to the full from economies of scale

Government policy and monopoly

If the benefits of monopoly exceed the costs of monopoly, the government may decide to allow monopoly to survive. Conversely, if the costs of monopoly exceed any likely benefits, the government may try to break up an established monopoly and prevent the formation of new monopolies. Nevertheless, even when the decision is made to allow a monopoly, there is still a case for government intervention to regulate the monopoly in order to prevent the firm abusing its market power in the future.

Examination skills

The skills most likely to be tested by objective-test or data-response questions on monopolies and resource allocation are:
- Identifying causes of monopoly and monopoly power.
- Applying key theoretical concepts such as productive efficiency and economies of scale to the analysis of monopoly.
- Explaining how a monopoly may adversely affect resource allocation.
- Drawing and explaining a diagram to show a monopoly restricting output and raising the price.
- Drawing and explaining a diagram to show a monopoly benefiting from economies of scale.
- Evaluating the costs and benefits of monopoly.

Examiner tip

At AS, exam questions may require analysis and evaluation of the case against monopoly and the case justifying monopoly.

AQA AS Economics

Examination questions

You should expect up to two objective-test questions on monopolies and resource allocation. OTQ 9 in the Questions and Answers section of this Guide is a typical example. Because monopoly is an important cause of market failure, your knowledge and understanding of monopoly and market power are also likely to be tested by questions set on specification sections 3.1.4 (Market failure) and 3.1.5 (Government intervention in the market). DRQ 3 in the Questions and Answers section shows how your knowledge of monopoly may be tested by a data-response question set on related key concepts, such as economies of scale and efficiency. A DRQ could also be set on a market dominated by large firms in which the data provide evidence of market power. From an examiner's point of view, data showing a previously natural monopoly, such as telecommunications being opened up to competition, would provide a fruitful scenario for a data-response question.

Common examination errors

Commonly made mistakes on monopolies and the allocation of resources are:
- Confusing a pure monopoly (one firm only in a market) with a monopolistic market (in which there is a dominant firm, but also other firms).
- Asserting without any further justification that monopoly is always bad.
- Inability to distinguish between pure monopoly and monopoly power.
- Failure to identify monopoly as a cause of market failure.
- A lack of understanding of the significance of barriers to entry, which deter or prevent competition.
- Inability to apply key economic concepts such as productive efficiency to the analysis and evaluation of monopoly.
- Drifting into a long descriptive account of the causes of monopoly when the question requires analysis and evaluation of the effects of monopoly power.

Summary

- Pure monopoly occurs when there is only one firm in an industry or market.

- Monopolies are protected by barriers to entry which prevent new firms from entering the market.

- Monopoly power is strongest when a firm produces an essential good for which there are no substitutes.

- Natural monopoly occurs when there is room in the market for only one firm benefiting from full economies of scale.

- By restricting output and raising the price, monopoly results in resource misallocation. This provides the main case against monopoly.

- Monopolies also restrict choice and exercise producer sovereignty at the expense of consumers.

- However, monopolies may be able to benefit from economies of scale. If the resulting fall in average costs are passed on to consumers in the form of lower prices, monopoly can be justified.

- A monopoly may use its monopoly power and monopoly profit to finance innovation in new products and better ways of making existing products.

Government intervention in the market

These notes relate to AQA specification section 3.1.5 and prepare you to answer examination questions on:
- why governments intervene in markets
- the various ways in which governments intervene in markets
- the situation known as government failure, which arises when government intervention in markets is unsuccessful or creates new problems

Essential information

Why governments intervene in markets

This final topic in the specification for 'Unit 1: Markets and market failure' requires the application of many terms and concepts you have studied earlier in this Guide to the role of government in markets. Economists assume that governments intervene in markets to maximise the social welfare of the whole community, but like ordinary consumers and firms, governments face conflicts and trade-offs when trying to achieve their objectives.

At the microeconomic level, governments intervene in markets primarily to try to eliminate, or at least reduce, market failures that are deemed to be occurring, or to prevent the emergence of market failure in the future.

Government intervention to correct complete market failure

Complete market failure occurs when there is no market at all, or a missing market. In the case of missing markets associated with **public goods**, government intervention *replaces* the market, with the government providing goods such as roads and defence. There are also missing markets in externalities: for example, the negative externality associated with pollution and the positive externality created by people enjoying looking at a beautiful building. In these cases, governments can intervene to discourage production of the negative externality and to encourage property owners to look after their buildings.

Government intervention to correct partial market failure

By contrast, in the case of **partial market failure**, where markets *do* function, but prices signal the wrong information and create the wrong incentives, government intervention takes two rather different forms. These are:
- As is the case with government response to complete failure, the government may replace or abolish the market (e.g. direct state provision, financed out of general taxation, of merit goods such as state education and healthcare, together with the banning of markets in demerit goods, such as heroin and cocaine).

- Alternatively (or possibly in addition), governments try to **adjust prices** so as to correct or at least reduce the resource misallocation that unregulated or 'free' market forces are responsible for. Price adjustment occurs through the use of **indirect taxes, subsidies, maximum price laws (price ceilings), minimum price laws (price floors)** and **buffer stock intervention** in the market.

Two examples of government intervention

Figure 13 can be used to illustrate two different forms of government intervention in the market:

- the impact of minimum price legislation (a price floor)
- the operation of a buffer stock scheme for an agricultural good such as rubber or coffee

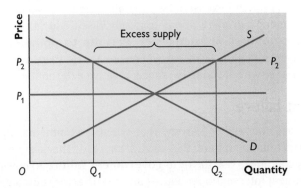

Figure 13 Effects of government intervention in the market

Using Figure 13 to analyse the effect of price controls, price P_2 can be viewed as a minimum legal price or floor price, imposed by the government, below which it is illegal to trade. The national minimum wage in the labour market is an example. In effect, government intervention distorts the price mechanism and prevents the price falling to the equilibrium P_1. The market fails to clear and excess supply persists.

To explain how Figure 13 can be used to illustrate a buffer stock scheme for a good such as coffee, we shall assume that a bumper harvest has previously shifted the supply curve to the position shown in the diagram. Because the market-clearing or equilibrium price P_1 is deemed too low, the government (or some other authority) sets an intervention price P_2 and begins support buying to take the excess supply off the market. Quantity $Q_2 - Q_1$ goes into a buffer stock, which may eventually be sold if a bad harvest shifts supply to the left and raises the price to an unacceptably high level.

Regulation, indirect taxation and subsidies

Regulation, indirect taxation and subsidies are perhaps the most important policy instruments that governments use to achieve their objectives and to correct partial market failure.

Regulation

Regulation is used in a number of ways in order to:

- deter monopoly abuse
- force people to consume merit goods (e.g. car seat belts)

Knowledge check 23

How does a price ceiling affect a market?

indirect taxation a tax imposed by the government on producers or firms, some of which is passed on to consumers as a price rise.

subsidy money given by the government to producers or firms, who use the subsidy to reduce the price that consumers pay.

Knowledge check 24

How can the use of regulation control the emission of negative externalities?

Knowledge check 25

Distinguish between the signalling and incentive functions of prices.

Examiner tip

See OTQ 7 in the Questions and Answers section of this Guide for an example of a question testing analysis of the impact of an indirect tax on a market.

Examiner tip

Make sure you don't confuse government failure and market failure.

- restrict consumption of demerit goods
- control the emission of negative externalities
- promote positive externalities

Indirect taxation and subsidies

Indirect taxes (and their opposite, subsidies) work in a rather different way. Whereas regulations place boundaries on the way markets can work, and thereby constrain how the market functions, indirect taxes and subsidies alter prices *within* the market. Indirect taxes and subsidies affect the **signalling function** of prices and the **incentives** that prices create for consumers and firms. Indirect taxes are commonly used by governments, alongside regulation, to discourage consumption of demerit goods such as tobacco and, illustrating the **polluter must pay** principle, to punish firms and motorists for the externalities they discharge. Subsidies can be used to encourage consumption of merit goods (e.g. subsidised education and healthcare) and the production of positive externalities. **Permits to pollute**, which in effect create a market (in pollution licences) where previously there was no market for pollution, are another way of trying to reduce negative externalities.

Government failure

Students often assume, rather naively, that when governments intervene in the economy to correct market failure, they always succeed. This is simply not the case, and nowadays economists use the term **government failure** to cover all situations in which government intervention produces an unsatisfactory outcome. Government failures range from the relatively trivial, when intervention is ineffective but where harm is restricted to the cost of resources used up and wasted by the intervention, to cases when intervention produces new and much more serious problems that did not exist before. For example, banning alcohol promotes the growth of illegal and criminal underground markets in which the social costs of consumption may be far worse than in a legal market. As the specification states: *'governments may create rather than remove market distortions; inadequate information, conflicting objectives and administrative costs should be recognised as possible sources of government failure.'*

Examination skills

The skills most likely to be tested by objective-test or data-response questions on governments and markets are:
- Identifying the many different ways in which governments can intervene in markets.
- Drawing supply and demand diagrams to illustrate the effect of government intervention in markets.
- Relating government intervention to the correction of market failures.
- Appreciating that intervention may not be successful and that problems of government failure may result.
- Evaluating the case for, or the effects of, intervention.
- Discussing the effects of reduced intervention (e.g. through deregulation or through abandoning a method of intervention), rather than increased intervention.

Examination questions

OTQ 9 in the Questions and Answers section of this Guide tests understanding of government intervention through imposing indirect taxes in markets.

You should expect some aspect of government intervention in markets to figure in one or more of the wrong answers to some of the objective-test questions in the examination. Government intervention in markets is also quite likely to feature in at least one part of a data-response question. See DRQs 1 (03) and (04), 2(04), 4 (03) and (04), 5(03) and (04) and 6 (04) for examples.

Common examination errors

Commonly made mistakes on governments and markets are:
- Failure to relate intervention in markets to the government's objectives.
- Confusing the two main reasons why governments provide goods or services through state spending: because markets completely fail to provide public goods such as defence, and because they under-provide merit goods such as healthcare.
- Confusing objectives and methods of intervention.
- Describing methods of intervention when the question asks for evaluation of methods.
- Inability to use appropriate supply and demand diagrams to illustrate the effect of intervention.
- Assuming that government intervention is always successful and improves economic welfare.
- Failure to appreciate the many different ways in which governments can intervene, including state ownership and direct provision of goods and services.

Summary

- Governments intervene in markets to maximise the social welfare of the whole community.
- In doing so, governments face policy conflicts which may be resolved by trading-off between policy objectives.
- Governments intervene in markets to try to eliminate or reduce market failures and to prevent the emergence of market failure in the future.
- Governments can use a variety of policies to influence the price charged in a market, e.g. maximum and minimum price laws, buffer stock intervention, taxation and subsidy.
- Governments provide public goods because markets fail to provide pure public goods. The government replaces the market.
- Governments also replace the market by providing merit goods, though they also subsidise market provision.
- Governments ban production and consumption of some demerit goods, but tax others.
- Governments intervene in markets through regulation, taxes and subsidies.
- Attempts by government to correct market failure may lead to government failure.
- Government failure covers all situations in which government intervention produces an unsatisfactory outcome.

Questions & Answers

The ECON I exam

The ECON 1 exam is 1 hour 15 minutes long and has a maximum mark of 75. The exam paper contains two sections, A and B, both of which must be answered. **Section A**, which accounts for 25 marks (approximately 33% of the total), comprises 25 compulsory objective-test questions or OTQs. One mark will be awarded for each OTQ answered correctly. **Section B** accounts for 50 marks (approximately 67% of the total) and comprises two data-response questions (DRQs), labelled **Context 1** and **Context 2**, of which you should answer one.

The exam's assessment objectives

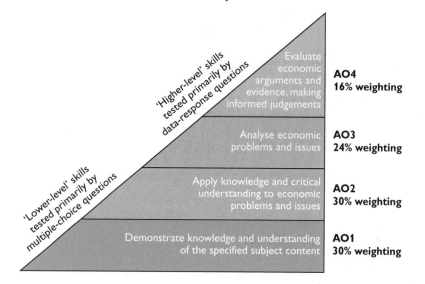

Figure 14 The examination's assessment objectives arranged along the incline of difficulty

The examination has four **assessment objectives (AOs)**, which are shown in Figure 14, together with their examination weightings, arranged in an incline of difficulty. 'Lower-level' skills of knowledge and factual recall are included in AO1 (at the bottom of the incline). Moving up the incline, increasingly 'higher-level' skills feature in the AOs: application of knowledge and critical understanding (AO2); analysis of problems (AO3); and evaluation of arguments and evidence (AO4). Overall, 60% of the examination questions are knowledge-based, testing the relatively 'lower-level' skills in AOs 1 and 2. The remaining 40% of examination questions meet AOs 3 and 4.

Answering objective-test questions

An objective-test question contains a 'stem' followed by four possible answers (A, B, C and D), only one of which is correct. Typically, OTQs are set to test students' ability to perform simple calculations and their knowledge of key definitions and concepts, especially on parts of the specification not covered by the data-response questions. OTQs primarily test the 'lower-level' skills related to knowledge and understanding in AOs 1 and 2. You should expect about ten of the 25 OTQs to test AO1, a further eight or nine to test AO2 and the remaining questions to test AO3, the analysis of economic problems and issues. AO4, centring on the skill of evaluation, is *not* tested in the objective-test question section of the examination paper.

Answering data-response questions

Whereas the 25 OTQs in Section A of the examination paper are compulsory, Section B comprises two data-response questions of which you must answer one. As mentioned earlier, the DRQs are numbered as Context 1 and Context 2. Each Context question contains four sub-questions, listed as [01], [02], [03] and [04] for Context 1, and [05], [06], [07] and [08] for Context 2. The mark allocation for the four parts of each question is [01] and [05]: 5 marks; [02] and [06]: 8 marks; [03] and [07]: 12 marks; and [04] and [08]: 25 marks. The total mark for each data-response question is 50.

The layout and structure of the questions will be similar to the six data-response questions which complete this Guide. Each question is likely to contain two or three sets of data. When, for example, three data sets are used in both questions, they will be labelled **Extract A**, **Extract B** and **Extract C** for Context 1, and **Extract D**, **Extract E** and **Extract F** for Context 2. In each question, one set of data is likely to be numerical: for example, a line graph, a bar graph, a pie graph or a table. Text or passage data presented in AQA data-response questions generally resemble an extract taken from a newspaper article: for example, an article in the *Financial Times*, the *Independent* or *The Economist*. Numerical data may be taken from a government source, which will be indicated below the graph or table used in the question. The Office for National Statistics (ONS) is a common source for numerical data used in an ECON 1 data-response question.

Both DRQs will be structured in exactly the same way and test the same assessment objectives. The questions are supposed to be equally difficult, but in practice almost every student finds one question more attractive than the other. Whichever question you initially favour, don't rush your choice of question. Careful thought and a sensible final decision are necessary if you are to do yourself full justice. You don't want to realise 10 minutes into your answer for Context 2 that you can't answer part [08] and that it is too late to switch to Context 1.

An 'incline of difficulty' will always be built into the DRQs, with the earlier parts of each question being the most straightforward. The first three parts of each DRQ will be marked using an **issue-based mark scheme** which lists the marks that can be awarded for the particular issues (and associated development) that might be included in the answer.

The last part of each DRQ differs from the earlier parts in three significant ways. First, and most obviously, parts [04] and [08] carry significantly more marks than the earlier parts of the questions — 50% of the total marks for the question and a third of the total marks for the whole paper. If you time the examination incorrectly and fail to develop your answer to part [04] or [08] beyond a cursory footnote, you will reduce considerably your chance of achieving a grade A. Second, whereas the earlier parts of the questions should be answered quite briefly, you are expected to write an extended answer of several paragraphs for parts [04] and [08]. You should think of this as a 'mini' essay. Third, 'higher-level' skills are expected. Because of this, a completely different type of mark scheme, known as a **levels of response mark scheme**, is used for parts [04] and [08] of each DRQ. It is vital to familiarise yourself with this mark scheme and to bear it in mind when you practise data-response questions.

The first two parts of each DRQ test primarily the 'lower-level' skills set in AOs 1 and 2. Parts [03] and [07] focus mainly on the 'higher-level' skill of analysis (AO3). Finally, parts [04] and [08] test the evaluation skills embodied in AO4.

The four key skills

Knowledge and understanding

With respect to the two lower-order skills of **knowledge** and **understanding**, AQA requires you to show an awareness of economic terminology and theories relevant to the Unit 1 specification. You must also show awareness of real-world issues, especially those relevant to the UK. Your knowledge and understanding will be tested in the exam by most of the 25 objective-test questions in Section A of the paper. For Section B (the data-response questions) as well as for Section A, you are expected to understand market theory, particularly supply and demand theory and related concepts such as elasticity. You must know about real-world markets: for example, primary product markets, real-world market failures such as externalities and public goods, and events that have occurred in UK markets in recent years, e.g. in the housing market. Finally you must understand how events in world markets impact on UK markets, such as rising world food prices.

Application

In Section B of the exam paper, the third part of each data-response question typically starts with the word 'Explain'. **Application** requires the selection of an appropriate theory or set of theories from the intellectual toolkit stored in your brain to explain an issue or issues posed by the question. The issue may centre on the *causes* of an economic problem, or the *effects* of the problem. Application of your knowledge of events that are happening, or which have recently happened, in the economy is also required.

Analysis

Analysis requires selection of relevant information from the data source(s) and then the use of the selected information, perhaps as evidence, in your answer. Information in the data is there to provide a *prompt* or *prompts* for the answer. You should indicate which bits of the data you are using, mentioning the Extract and the line numbers, without at the same time resorting to 'copying out' sentences or numbers from the data.

Evaluation

Evaluation is the higher-order skill which separates good answers that earn an A or B grade for the data-response question from those that at best reach grade C. Evaluation is also the skill which exam students find it most difficult to display.

To evaluate, you need to demonstrate a critical approach to economic models and methods of enquiry: for example, the assumption underlying market theory that market forces always tend to eliminate excess demand or excess supply to quickly establish equilibrium. You should also demonstrate the ability to produce reasoned conclusions clearly and concisely and to assess the strengths and weaknesses of economic arguments and limitations of the data in the question.

Competing theories or explanations often lead into evaluation. Evaluation can require you to explain why, in your view, some arguments or lines of reasoning are more important than others. Where appropriate, alternative and competing theories and viewpoints must be weighed up. The assumptions you are making should be stated, considered and sometimes questioned.

The effects of different types of government intervention in markets must be judged, sometimes exploring their possible 'knock-on' and 'feedback' effects induced elsewhere in the economy. Very often a part [04] or [08] asks for consideration of the **advantages** and **disadvantages** of, or the **costs** and **benefits** of, or the **case for** versus the **case against** a course of action mentioned in the question.

Good evaluation requires you to **prioritise** the evidence and arguments you introduce into your answer. One way to do this is to explain, when introducing each of the points or arguments you are making, whether in your view it is significant *always*, significant but *only under a particular set of assumptions*, or though relevant, rather trivial. When making such points, your answer must go beyond mere assertion, i.e. you must **justify** your arguments and use evidence.

Finally, there are two different ways of evaluating, but in my view the first way is better than the second. My preferred way of evaluating, as indicated above, is to assess the strengths and weaknesses of each argument as you bring it into your answer. If you organise your answer in this way, make sure that every time you introduce a new argument you start a new paragraph. It is also a good idea to leave a vacant line between paragraphs so that the examiner's eye is drawn to the fact that a new argument is being presented.

The second way to evaluate is to leave it all to the final concluding paragraph. At its worst, so-called evaluation presented in the concluding paragraph can boil down merely to a statement such as, 'in my view, the case for is therefore stronger than the case against'. Unfortunately such a concluding statement is not evaluation, it is unjustified assertion. Good evaluation in a concluding paragraph must always refer back to arguments used earlier in the answer, making a clear final judgement as to which arguments, if any, are most important. Perhaps the best approach to organising your answer is to combine the two methods of evaluation: namely, evaluate each point as you develop your answer before concluding with a winding-up paragraph that presents an 'overview' or summary of the arguments you believe to be most important.

Finally, it is worth remembering that AQA draws students' attention to a significant distinction between **weak** and **strong** evaluation. Weak evaluation consists of assertions largely unsupported by either evidence or any accompanying analysis. By contrast, strong evaluation uses sound economic analysis to support the conclusions being drawn, plus evidence from the real world.

Evaluation and levels of skill mark schemes

According to AQA mark schemes, however good the analysis, an answer devoid of evaluation cannot climb above **Level 2** in the mark scheme (4 to 9 marks). Likewise an answer with some evaluation but no analytical use of economic theory is constrained to Level 2. (Such answers are sometimes called 'General Studies' answers.) A **Level 3** answer (10 to 16 marks out of the 25 available marks) must be a reasonable response, including some correct analysis but very limited or weak evaluation. A **Level 4** answer (17 to 21 marks) must include either some good and correct analysis but very limited evaluation, or reasonable analysis and reasonable evaluation. Finally, the highest level, **Level 5** (22 to 25 marks) requires both good analysis and good or strong evaluation, with final evaluation evident in a concluding paragraph.

A strategy for tackling the examination

(1) On opening the examination booklet, turn immediately to the second section and spend up to 5 minutes reading *both* DRQs.

(2) Then go back to the first section and spend up to 20 minutes answering the 25 OTQs, completing your first run through the questions. While you are doing this, you will be subconsciously thinking about the DRQs.

(3) Read through both DRQs again, paying particular attention to whether you can write a good answer to parts [04] and [08] of each question, the parts that carry the most marks.

(4) After careful thought, make your final choice and spend about 50 minutes answering *all* the parts of the DRQ. Take account of the marks indicated in brackets for each sub-question when allocating the 50 minutes between each part of the question. Make sure you spend over half the time answering part [04] or [08].

(5) In the last 5 minutes of the examination, complete a second run through the OTQs and read through your written answers to check for and correct mistakes — including spelling and grammatical mistakes.

The exam questions in this Guide

The 25 examination-style questions that follow are designed to be a key learning, revision and exam preparation resource. There are 19 OTQs and six DRQs. The OTQs divide into two parts. Part 1 includes nine OTQs and each question is typical of questions asked on one of the nine topics covered in the Content Guidance section of this Guide. Each of these questions is similar in layout, structure and style to an OTQ in the ECON 1 examination paper. A commentary has been included after each question to explain the correct answer and any other important features of the question. Part 2 contains ten OTQs, chosen to represent types of question that regularly catch out unwary students.

For these questions, the commentary after each question explains the nature of the pitfall that may catch you out.

The 19 OTQs are followed by six DRQs. You can use the DRQs either as timed test questions in the lead-up to the examination or to reinforce your understanding of the specification subject matter, topic by topic, as you proceed through the Content Guidance. In this book, the data-response questions are numbered 1 to 6, but in the AQA exam you will eventually sit, the two questions will be numbered Context 1 and Context 2.

This section covering the DRQs also includes:
- a student's answer for each DRQ
- examiner's comments on each student's answer explaining, where relevant, how the answer could be improved. These comments are denoted by the icon ⓔ.

Understanding UMS marks

It is important to understand the difference between the two types of marks that the GCE examining boards award for students' work: **raw marks** and **uniform mark scale (UMS)** marks.

For the data-response questions, raw marks are the marks out of 50 awarded by the examiner who reads your script. These marks are added to the marks achieved for the 25 objective-test questions, to give an overall maximum total of 75 marks. After all the scripts have been marked, and basing their decisions only on raw marks, a grade-awarding panel decides where the grade boundaries should be set for each of the AS pass grades: A, B, C, D and E.

After all the grade boundaries have been set as raw marks, e.g. 55 out of 75 for a grade A, each student's raw mark for the ECON 1 paper is converted into a UMS mark. Uniform mark scale marks have the same grade boundaries — for all subjects and all unit exams. These are: **grade A: 80%; grade B: 70%; grade C: 60%; grade D: 50%; grade E: 40%**.

The marks awarded for students' answers for each of the DRQs in the following pages are raw marks and not UMS marks. It must be stressed that the actual raw mark at which a particular grade boundary is set varies from examination to examination, depending on a number of factors. The factors include: judgement as to whether the questions in the ECON 1 exam were relatively easy or difficult in comparison with the questions set in previous examinations; and the **statistically recommended mark** for a particular grade, which is determined by computer analysis of the marks earned at GCSE a year earlier by the cohort of students taking the ECON 1 exam.

Objective-test questions

Questions on Topics 1 to 9

ⓔ The nine objective-test questions that follow provide examples of questions typical of those set on each of the nine topics in the Contents Guidance section of this Guide. Each OTQ is followed by a short commentary explaining the correct answer and any other matter relevant to avoiding choosing a wrong answer (known as a distracter).

Question 1: the economic problem

Which of the following is a positive economic statement?

A Education should be made available free for all children

B Governments ought to intervene in the economy to correct market failures

C A reduction in welfare benefits will increase the supply of labour

D Imposing price controls is an unfair method of allocating resources

ⓔ It is sensible to expect one question in each examination on the distinction between positive and normative statements. A positive statement is a statement of fact or definition (e.g. a metre contains 100 centimetres); or it is an assertion or prediction that may or may not be true, but which can be tested to see if it is true or false. For this question, **C** is a positive statement and thus the correct answer. **A**, **B**, and **D** are all normative statements. Note the give-away words: 'should', 'ought' and 'unfair' which indicate the statement of opinion and value judgement in each of the statements.

Question 2: supply and demand in competitive markets

Which of the following events might cause the demand curve for chicken meat to shift to the right?

A a fall in the price of chicken meat

B a fall in the price of turkey meat

C an outbreak of salmonella infection in chicken meat

D the publication of a health report urging people to eat white rather than red meats

ⓔ This question tests knowledge of the causes of shifts in demand. The correct answer is **D**: the publication of the health report specified in the question would alter people's behaviour in favour of eating chicken and turkey (white meats) and away from red meats such as beef and lamb. The demand curve for chicken meat would therefore shift rightward. Although the question does not ask about the demand curves for red meats, the demand curves for beef and lamb would shift to the left.

Question 3: elasticity

The table below shows estimates of elasticities of demand for apples and oranges taken from the National Food Survey.

| | Elasticity with respect to: | | |
	price of apples	price of oranges	income
Apples	−0.29	−0.07	+0.32
Oranges	−0.16	−1.33	+0.14

Which of the following can be concluded from the data?

A Apples and oranges are substitutes for each other

B Apples but not oranges are inferior goods

C The demand for apples is both price inelastic and income inelastic

D The demand for oranges is both price elastic and income elastic

ⓔ The cross elasticity of demand for apples with respect to the price of oranges is −0.07 while that for oranges with respect to the price of apples is −0.16. Both cross elasticities are negative, indicating that apples and oranges are in joint demand rather than substitutes. **A** is therefore wrong. **B** is also wrong as both goods have positive income elasticities of demand (+0.32 and +0.14 respectively) and are therefore normal goods. **C** is the correct answer: the price and income elasticities of demand for apples are both less than 1 (ignoring the minus sign for the price elasticity). The first part of statement **D** is correct, demand for oranges being price elastic, but the second part is wrong: demand for oranges is income inelastic.

Question 4: prices and resource allocation

All the following statements about the role of prices in a market economy are true except one. **Which statement is the odd one out?**

A Prices convey information which helps consumers decide what to buy

B High prices justify monopoly profit

C Changing prices of capital and labour lead to firms changing methods of production

D Changing prices may result in a different allocation of resources

ⓔ This question is about the three functions that prices perform in markets. Statements **A**, **C** and **D** are respectively about the signalling, incentive and rationing functions of prices. This leaves **B** as the odd one out and the correct answer. High prices can lead to monopoly profit, but this does not justify monopoly profit.

Question 5: production and efficiency

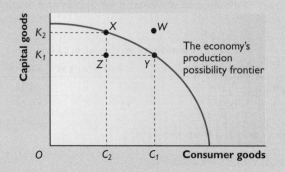

The economy's production possibility frontier

Which of the following statements relating to the production possibility frontier is NOT correct?

A The opportunity cost of increasing the output of capital goods from K_1 to K_2 is sacrificed output of consumer goods of $C_1 - C_2$

B Point W is more productively efficient than points X, Y and Z

C Point Z is productively inefficient

D Available economic resources are fully employed at points X and Y

(e) Productive efficiency can be illustrated on a production possibility frontier as well as on an average cost diagram. A production possibility curve or frontier is one of the most useful diagrams in economics, and a favourite for objective-test questions. You must always be extra careful when, as in this question, you are asked to identify the odd one out, i.e. the *untrue* statement. It is so easy to read the question hurriedly and to choose the first *true* statement as the answer. In this question, **A**, **C** and **D** are true, and therefore *not* the answer. **B**, the only untrue statement, is the answer. While points X and Y are productively efficient, point W is not. W is located outside or beyond the production possibility frontier and is therefore unattainable.

Question 6: market failure, public goods and externalities

Which of the following statements about public goods is correct?

A Public goods are defined as those goods provided by the state

B Public goods are examples of 'free goods'

C Public goods are characterised by the 'free-rider' problem

D The problem of scarcity does not affect the provision of public goods

(e) A public good such as national defence or street lighting possesses the characteristic of non-excludability which creates the 'free-rider' problem. This means that **C** is the answer. If a public good is provided for one person, it is provided for all in the sense that it is impossible to exclude other people from receiving the good's benefits. As a result, many people may be tempted to 'free-ride' (a 'free-rider' being a person who benefits without paying), which in turn causes the incentive function of prices to break down. The ability to charge a price provides the incentive for entrepreneurs to provide goods through markets. However, when people can benefit without paying, the incentive function of prices breaks down because private entrepreneurs cannot sell the goods profitably. In extreme cases, complete market failure results, i.e. the market collapses completely, resulting in a 'missing market'.

Question 7: merit and demerit goods, income and wealth inequalities and labour immobility

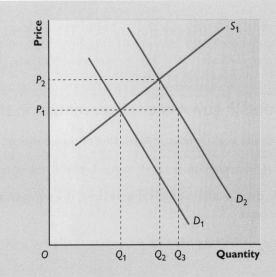

The graph above depicts the market for a merit good such as healthcare. If the government wishes to stabilise the price of healthcare at P_1, following a shift to the right of the demand curve from D_1 to D_2, it should:

A subsidise healthcare

B provide healthcare solely through state spending

C impose a minimum price or price floor of P_1

D take action to eliminate the excess supply of healthcare at price P_2

ⓔ The graph shows market forces raising the price of healthcare from P_1 to P_2. To prevent the price rising, producers must be subsidised to bring the price down once again to P_1. Statement **A** therefore provides the correct answer. Statement **B** bypasses the issue of whether a price would be charged or whether healthcare would be provided at zero price, whereas **D** is nonsense as the shift of the demand curve to the right results in excess *demand* at price P_1 rather than excess *supply*. Imposing a minimum price of P_1 (statement **C**) would have no effect, since, without a subsidy, trading takes place at P_2 which is above P_1.

Question 8: monopolies and the allocation of resources

For society as a whole, monopoly may be preferable to a competitive market whenever:

A the monopoly restricts output and raises the price

B fewer resources end up being devoted to research and development

C consumer choice is reduced

D economies of scale reduce average production costs

ⓔ What is preferable for society as a whole may of course be different from what is preferable for the owners of the monopoly. **D** is the correct answer because economies of scale provide one of the two main justifications of monopoly, the other being the use of monopoly profit to finance research and development. The other possible answers focus on the case *against* monopoly rather than the case that can justify monopoly.

Question 9: government intervention in the economy

Which of the following is an example of government regulation of the economy?

A The government selling a state-owned industry such as Air Traffic Control to private ownership

B The government announcing the abolition of rules that restrict the number of commercial radio stations allowed by law to operate

C The government encouraging the General Medical Council to discipline professionally negligent doctors

D A legal requirement enforced by local authorities that seat belts be fitted in all coaches and mini-buses

ⓔ This question is testing knowledge of methods of government intervention in the market economy. Statement **A** is an example of *privatisation* rather than *regulation*, so it is not the answer. Statement **B** is also wrong, being an example of *deregulation* or the abolition of previously imposed rules or regulations. Statement **C** does provide an example of regulation, *self-regulation* by the members of a profession, albeit with government encouragement, rather than external regulation of the profession by the government. This leaves statement **D** as the answer. According to the statement, the regulation has been imposed by central government and enforced by local government.

Questions that can trick you

The ten objective-test questions that follow have been chosen to represent types of question that regularly catch out unwary students. For these questions, the commentary with each question explains the nature of the pitfall in the question that may catch you out.

Question 1 Look out for 'weasel words' such as 'most likely', 'inevitably' and 'always'

ⓔ Sometimes, the first sentence of an objective-test question, which is called the **stem**, contains 'weasel words' such as 'most likely', 'inevitably' and 'always'. The words 'most likely', which appear in this question, mean that more than one of the possible answers could be correct, but one is 'more correct' than the others. In this case, **D** is the correct answer as the statement indicates that market failure is occurring. In this situation, government intervention is most likely to correct or reduce the market failure. Because the other statements do not give examples of market failure, it is less likely that government intervention can improve on the market and hence improve resource allocation.

> **Intervention by the government in a market economy is most likely to improve resource allocation if**
>
> **A** a shortage has caused a product's price to rise
>
> **B** fewer resources end up being devoted to research and development
>
> **C** firms reduce production in response to a fall in demand
>
> **D** the market is over-supplying a product that produces a negative externality

Question 2 Look out for the words 'except' and 'not' in the stem of a question

ⓔ The stem of an objective-test question may be worded, 'Which of the following statements is **not** true?' All too often, students do not read the question carefully and choose the first *correct* answer, even though the chosen answer should be the *incorrect* alternative. Likewise, as in the question below, look out for the word 'except' in the question.

> **Economies of scale can result from all the following *except* one. Which is the exception?**
>
> **A** A factory employs two shifts of workers rather than one shift per day to make better use of fixed capacity
>
> **B** A bus company replaces smaller buses with larger buses
>
> **C** An increase in the size of a firm's capacity and plant
>
> **D** Increased firm size allowing the firm to employ specialist managers

(e) For this question, statements **B**, **C** and **D** are all correct, so do not provide the answer. The words 'fixed capacity' in the first statement indicate that **A** is the exception and therefore the correct answer. Economies of scale are defined as falling average costs when the scale of the firm increases. **A** is untrue because the size of the fixed capacity does not change.

Question 3 Failure to appreciate the meaning of market failure

(e) Exam students often believe that when a good's price suddenly rises, this must illustrate market failure. More often than not it is nothing of the sort. Instead, it is simply the market adjusting to a new equilibrium following an event such as a drought which shifts supply to the left, or a sudden increase in demand which shifts the demand curve to the right. Consider the following question:

Market failure arises if

A a good's price rises in response to excess demand

B firms fail to make profits

C positive externalities exist in production

D government intervention makes the market perform badly

(e) Statements **A** and **B** do not in themselves indicate that market failure is occurring. Statement **D** indicates that government failure rather than market failure is taking place, so this possible answer is also wrong. This leaves **C** as the correct answer.

Question 4 Failure to appreciate the meaning of government failure

(e) Following on from Question 3, many students confuse government failure with market failure. Whereas market failure occurs when markets perform unsatisfactorily, or fail to function at all, government failure occurs when government intervention in a market in an attempt to correct market failure makes things worse rather than better.

Government failure must occur when

A the government decides not to intervene in the market

B social benefits are less than social costs

C government intervention leads to a net welfare loss compared to a free market outcome

D people suffer from negative externalities

(e) In the question above, **B** and **D** are irrelevant to the question. The word 'must' in the stem of the question means that **A** is wrong. This leaves **C** as the correct answer, with the statement providing a neat illustration of government failure.

Question 5 Dealing with the concept of productivity

ⓔ Productivity is one of the most important concepts in both the Unit 1 and Unit 2 specifications, and one which students often fail to understand, confusing productivity with production. Usually when economists talk about productivity they mean labour productivity, or output per worker. Objective-test questions often ask you to identify a cause of an increase in labour productivity. In the question below, statements **A**, **B** and **D** *could* lead to an increase in labour productivity, but as **C** states the most likely cause, it is the correct answer.

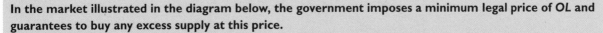

Which one of the following is most likely to lead to greater labour productivity in an industry?

A   **an increase in the number of producers in the industry**

B   **a fall in wages**

C   **firms adopting more capital-intensive methods of production**

D   **the demand curve in the market shifts to the right**

Question 6 How a price floor affects a market

ⓔ Objective-test questions are often set on price floors (minimum legal prices) or price ceilings (maximum legal prices). Students often make mistakes with this type of question by wrongly believing that minimum and maximum legal prices are prices that firms *must* charge. As the question below illustrates, a minimum legal price or price floor only affects or distorts a market if the price is set *above* the equilibrium or market-clearing price. By contrast, a maximum legal price or price ceiling has to be set below the equilibrium price for the market to be distorted.

In the market illustrated in the diagram below, the government imposes a minimum legal price of *OL* and guarantees to buy any excess supply at this price.

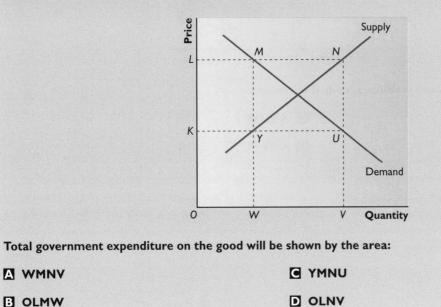

Total government expenditure on the good will be shown by the area:

A   **WMNV**   **C**   **YMNU**

B   **OLMW**   **D**   **OLNV**

ⓔ The minimum legal price imposed by the government, *OL*, is above the equilibrium price: namely, the price located at the intersection of the supply and demand curves. Because the minimum legal price is set *above* the equilibrium price, excess supply occurs in the market. Since the government guarantees to take the excess supply off the market, its total expenditure (amount bought, multiplied by the price paid) is shown by the area *WMNV*. The correct answer is therefore **A**.

Question 7 How an indirect tax affects a market

ⓔ Many, perhaps most, exam students experience difficulty when answering a question on an indirect tax or a subsidy. Indirect taxes or expenditure taxes imposed on firms are one of the factors that cause supply curves to shift upward or leftward. From the firms' point of view, the tax is equivalent to a rise in the costs of production. Just as with a cost increase, firms will try to pass the tax on to consumers by raising the price of the good. However, firms' ability to **shift the incidence** of the tax by raising the price is limited by the elasticity of the demand curve. Except in the special case when demand is completely inelastic, demand falls as the price is raised. Study the question below:

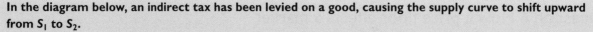

In the diagram below, an indirect tax has been levied on a good, causing the supply curve to shift upward from S_1 to S_2.

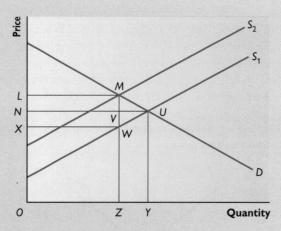

The amount of tax borne by the producers is equal to the area:

A XLMW

C XNUW

B NLMV

D XNVW

ⓔ In the example depicted in the question, the firms can increase the price to *OL*, at which quantity *OZ* is bought and sold, but no higher. The total tax paid to the government is shown by the rectangle *XLMW*. This divides into two smaller rectangles, *NLMV* and *XNVW*, which lie respectively above and below *ON*, which was the equilibrium price *before* the tax was imposed.

NLMV is the part of the tax passed on to consumers as a price rise (the shifted incidence of the tax), whereas XNVW must be borne by the producers (the unshifted incidence of the tax). XNVW is the correct answer: statement **D**.

Question 8 Calculating private, external and social benefits and costs

ⓔ The question below requires calculation of benefits and costs from the information provided in the question. Although social benefits and/or social costs are mentioned in three of the four possible answers, neither is shown explicitly in the data in the question. It is up to you to know that social benefits and costs are respectively the sum of private and external benefits and costs.

The positive and negative externalities of building a new nuclear power station are shown below.

Private benefits £260 million	Private costs £220 million
External benefits £40 million	External costs £60 million

It can be concluded that the:

A nuclear power station will not be profitable

B social benefits exceed the social costs

C social benefits are less than the private benefits

D social costs are £160 million

ⓔ Social benefits are defined as private benefits plus external benefits. Likewise, social costs are private costs plus external costs. Adding up the two columns shows that social benefits are £300 million and social costs are £280 million. As a result the correct answer is **B**.

Question 9 Comparing a competitive market with a monopoly

ⓔ The section on markets in the Unit 1 specification concentrates mostly on competitive markets, with monopoly creeping in as a bit of an after-thought. Exam questions may ask you to compare a competitive market with a monopoly. The diagram in the question that follows shows how a monopoly can exploit consumers by restricting output and hiking up the price. Other questions may use a cost curve to show one of the possible benefits of monopoly: namely, how large size enables a monopoly to pass on to consumers as lower prices the lower average costs gained by benefiting from economies of scale.

The diagram below shows the prices charged and the levels of output produced in an industry under both competitive and monopoly conditions.

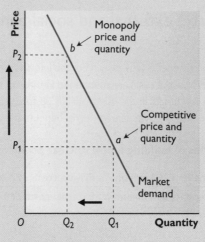

Which of the following can be concluded from the diagram?

A Compared to the competitive market, the monopoly restricts output and raises the price

B The competitive firms are productively efficient but the monopoly is productively inefficient

C The larger the number of competitive firms in the market, the greater the economies of scale

D The monopoly is a natural monopoly

ⓔ The correct answer is **A**. The diagram depicts the main argument against monopoly: namely, that when monopoly replaces a competitive market containing many firms, the monopoly hikes up the price it charges and reduces the level of output it produces. We cannot read anything about productive efficiency and natural monopoly into the graph, so **B** and **D** are wrong. Finally, **C** is incorrect because real-world markets are seldom large enough to contain a large number of competitive firms, with each benefiting from economies of scale.

Question 10 Markets in permits to pollute

ⓔ People who breathe in atmospheric pollution cannot charge the polluters who emit the pollution a market price for the negative externality they unwillingly consume. This is because there are missing markets in externalities. To try to mimic the incentive function of prices, surrogate markets have been created in which permits to pollute, or emissions quotas, are traded. Exam students often find it difficult to cope with questions that test knowledge of how such markets operate. The following is a typical example of such a question.

To reduce acid rain pollution discharged by power stations, the USA has set up a market in tradable pollution permits. Which of the following statements about pollution permits is *untrue*?

A Pollution permits involve the 'polluter must pay' principle

B Pollution permits involve some 'command and control'

C All affected power stations suffer financial penalties for polluting

D The permits create incentives for power stations to reduce pollution

ⓔ The system of pollution permits imposes a maximum pollution limit which has been reduced over a series of years. Since this involves 'command and control' regulation, statement **B** is true. Power stations that reduce pollution by more than the limit requires can sell their 'spare' pollution permits to power stations that fail to comply, to enable the latter to continue to pollute within the law. This is an example of the 'polluter must pay' principle, so statement **A** is also true. The same is the case for statement **D**, since the market creates incentives to reduce pollution to avoid the need to purchase 'spare' pollution permits. This leaves **C** as the only untrue statement and therefore the answer: under-complying power stations suffer financial penalty but the over-complying power stations that sell their 'spare' permits make a financial gain.

Data-response questions

Question I **The rice market**

Total for this question: 50 marks

Study Extracts A, B and C, and then answer all parts of the question that follows.

Extract A:

Australian production of rice and grapes for making wine, 1992–2008

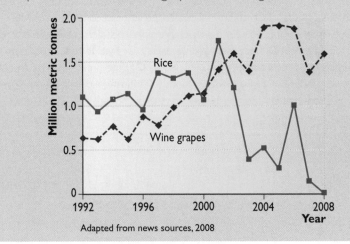

Adapted from news sources, 2008

Extract B:

Rice and wine production in Australia

The collapse of Australia's rice production, caused by six years of drought, is one of the factors contributing to a doubling of world rice prices. Drought has led to significant changes in Australia's agricultural heartland. Some farmers are abandoning rice, which requires large amounts of water, to plant less water-intensive crops, particularly wine grapes. Other rice farmers have sold fields or water rights, 5 usually to grape growers. Even with the recent doubling of rice prices, to around $1,000 a metric ton for the high rice grades produced by Australia, farmers find it more profitable to grow wine grapes. All told, wine grapes produce a profit of close to $2,000 an acre, while rice produces a profit of only $240 an acre. 'But rice is a staple food', says one commentator. 'Wine is not.' 10

Adapted from news sources

Extract C:

The rising price of rice

Rice is a staple food in the diets of nearly half the world's population. Dramatically rising prices and a growing fear of scarcity have prompted some of the world's largest rice producers to announce drastic limits on the amount of rice they export.

Governments across Asia and in many rice-consuming countries in Africa have long worried that a steep increase in prices could set off an angry reaction among low-income city dwellers. 5

Several factors are contributing to the steep rise in prices. Rising affluence in India and China has increased demand. At the same time, drought and other forms of bad weather have reduced output in Australia and elsewhere. Many rice farmers are turning to more lucrative cash crops, reducing the amount of land devoted to the 10 grain, and urbanisation and industrialisation have cut into the land devoted to rice cultivation.

Until the last few years, the potential for rapid price swings was dampened by the tendency of many governments to hold very large rice stockpiles to ensure food security. But those stockpiles were costly to maintain. So governments have been 15 drawing them down as world rice consumption has outstripped production for most of the last decade.

The relatively small quantities of rice traded between countries, combined with small stockpiles, now mean that prices can move quickly in response to supply disruptions. At the same time, speculative buying of rice on the world rice market and hoarding 20 by retailers and consumers have contributed to rising prices.

Governments have been reluctant to impose low maximum fixed prices (price ceilings) on rice, for fear that farmers would hoard rice or not bother to grow as much as they could. Indeed, China, which is virtually self-sufficient in rice, has raised the minimum price it guarantees to farmers. 25

Adapted from news sources

---

[01]   Define the term 'profit' (Extract B, line 8).   (5 marks)

ⓔ Part [01] of an ECON 1 or ECON 2 data-response question always asks for a definition of a key economic term or concept. This is the same for the first part of a Context 2 question which is numbered [05]. In every case, a short, sharp and accurate definition, often presented in a single sentence, is enough to earn full marks.

---

[02]   Using the information in Extract A, identify two significant points of comparison between the production of rice and the production of wine grapes in Australia over the period shown.   (8 marks)

ⓔ The second part of a data-response question often asks students to identify two significant points of comparison between the two variables shown in the data over a given period. The data may be displayed in a graph or table. When answering this type of question, it is important not to stray beyond the relatively simple task in hand: namely, to provide two points of comparison, supported by statistical evidence from the graph or table.

[03] **With the help of an appropriate diagram, explain how a price ceiling imposed by governments in major rice-producing countries might affect world rice markets.** (12 marks)

ⓔ The third part of a data-response question on a market often asks students to use an appropriate diagram to support the written explanation then provided. More often than not, the diagram should be a supply and demand diagram.

[04] **Evaluate policies other than a price ceiling that a government might use in order to reduce the growing inequality between rich and poor caused by rising food prices.** (25 marks)

ⓔ Sixteen per cent of the total marks for the ECON 1 examination are given for the skill of **evaluation**, and all these marks are devoted to the final part of the chosen data-response question. The key instruction is likely to be 'evaluate', 'assess', or 'do you agree?' Evaluation is the skill that students find most difficult and which is generally necessary if a grade A is to be earned. In the AS examination, it is possible to achieve a grade A without displaying the skill of evaluation. However, to do this, you must perform very well in the objective-test part of the examination (which does not test evaluation) and in the first three parts of the data-response question. Generally, however, the students who can evaluate are the ones who gain the A grades.

Student answer

[01] Profit is the difference between the revenue a firm earns from selling its output and the costs it incurs when producing the output: **a**

profit = sales revenue – costs of production

Extract B quotes the profit made by an Australian farmer from the grapes he grows as $2,000 an acre. Sales revenue of $6,000 minus costs of $4,000 would lead to this figure. **b**

ⓔ **5/5 marks awarded.** For this question, students are asked to define the concept 'profit'. **a** In this case, the first sentence earns all the 5 available marks. **b** The student includes a second sentence in her answer which uses illustrative figures to support her definition, but avoids the temptation to develop her answer unnecessarily.

[02] There appears to be a negative or inverse relationship between the two variables over the whole of the data period from 1992 to 2008. Rice production was larger than wine grape production at the beginning of the 16-year period (about 1.1 million tons as against about 0.7 million tons), but was below wine production at the end of the period in 2008 (zero versus about 1.6 million tons).

The second point of comparison **a** I have identified is that the production of rice fluctuated more than production of wine grapes in the second part of the period from about 2000 onward. **b**

ⓔ **6/8 marks awarded.** The student sticks to answering the question and earns 6 of the available 8 marks. **a** The mark scheme for the second part of a question of this type allows full marks to be earned by providing two significant points of comparison, as long as the comparisons are over the period shown. **b** With this answer, 2 marks are lost because the second point of comparison (though correct) has not been supported from the data.

[03] My diagram **a** shows the world price of rice, determined by free-market forces, at P_1. **a** My diagram does not show how this price has been reached, namely through an increase in world demand for rice shifting the market demand curve to the right to the position shown in my diagram.

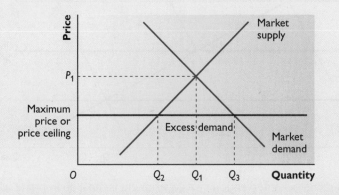

Governments in major rice-producing countries such as Vietnam have indeed tried to control the price of rice in their countries, but by imposing export restrictions rather than through price ceilings. For a price ceiling to reduce the price of rice, it must be set below the free-market price. But as my diagram shows, **b** excess demand then occurs (shown by the distance between Q_3 and Q_2). The resulting shortages **c** can lead to queues, waiting lists, black markets and corruption. People might of course respond to the shortage of rice by switching to alternative forms of food, though this may not be possible in countries where rice is the staple food. **c**

My last point is that the effect on world rice markets also depends on how the law is enforced or policed and what the punishments are for breaking the law. **c** Obviously, if price ceilings are not enforced, the effect on world rice markets will not be noticeable.

(e) **12/12 marks awarded.** The student writes a very good answer to this question, **a** drawing an accurate supply and demand diagram, **b** which is clearly explained. **c** The answer goes on to explain a number of effects of the price ceiling. The answer is well balanced between the diagram and the written explanation and does enough to earn all 12 marks.

[04] Rising food prices affect consumers in both developed and developing countries. In both types of economy the poor are adversely affected more than the rich, largely because expenditure on food forms a larger proportion of the income of the poor.

Governments can use many different policies, other than imposing price ceilings, to try to reduce food prices, and particularly those the poor have to pay. I shall discuss and evaluate three policies, namely buffer stock intervention, subsidies, and progressive taxation and transfers between income groups. **a**

First, buffer stock intervention. This can work in different ways, one of which I illustrate in the diagram below.

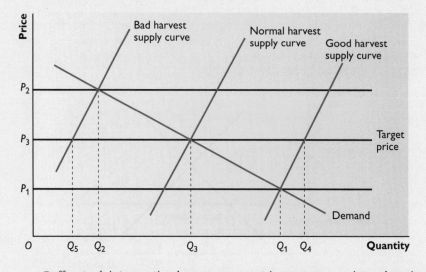

Buffer stock intervention by a government is most appropriate when, in a free market, food prices rise and fall from year to year because good harvests alternate with bad harvests. Suppose that a government decides to stabilise the price of an agricultural crop at the 'normal' year price, P_3. Following a good harvest, the government buys quantity Q_4 minus Q_3 to prevent the market price falling below P_3. But next year, following a bad harvest, the government supplements supply by releasing the product onto the market from the previously accumulated stock. The sale of Q_3 minus Q_5 prevents the price rising to P_2, and stabilises the price at P_3. The government, or an association of producers, accumulates a buffer stock when the harvest is good for releasing onto the market in the event of a crop failure. **b**

The problem with buffer stock intervention, in the context of the question, is that a stockpile of food has to be accumulated in the first place in order that the stock can later be released onto the market to dampen a rise in food prices. Unfortunately, as the information in Extract C indicates, food prices have risen for reasons additional to the effect of bad harvests, and governments do not currently possess surplus stocks that they can release onto the market. It must also be said that the release of buffer stocks onto the market can only stabilise the global price of food if intervention is taken by a large number of governments acting in tandem. Intervention by one government in isolation is unlikely to reduce food prices because one country, however large, is only a tiny part of the whole. **c**

Moving on to subsidies, these can be effective, but only in the countries which grant the subsidies. Subsidies are generally given to firms or producers, in this case farmers, but it is also possible to grant a subsidy direct to consumers. For example, a government could give rice or bread tokens to poor families which, when spent, would reduce the price of the foodstuff for the family. This could effectively reduce the price of food for poor people in the country involved, but by creating extra demand, it might actually increase the global free-market price of the subsidised foodstuffs. In the country granting the subsidy, a significant opportunity cost would be the other uses to which the money granted in subsidy could have been put. However, I think that subsidies paid directly to consumers should only be used as an essentially temporary form of intervention, largely because they distort the market mechanism, require high taxes to pay for them, and do little to encourage an increase in food production. **d**

My third policy option is using the tax and benefits systems to help the poor. By imposing progressive taxes on the better-off, in which the rich pay a larger proportion of their income in tax than the poor pay, and by paying out the tax revenue in benefits for the poor, the incomes of the poor can be raised so that they can afford to buy food, despite the increase in food prices. Besides the opportunity cost of the public spending involved (which is similar to that for subsidies, which I have already discussed), a disadvantage of such intervention could be its adverse effect on incentives. High taxes would punish the rich for working, while the transfer payments received by the poor would alter the choice between supplying labour and enjoying leisure (i.e. being unemployed) in favour of the latter.

However, my suggestions may not be very feasible, which brings me to my last point: as economists we should accept that prices must sometimes have to rise to create the incentives for people to change their economic behaviour. **e**

ⓔ 22/25 marks awarded. This is generally a superb answer which **a** analyses and evaluates a range of relevant policies. The answer sits at the bottom end of Level 5 (22 to 25 marks). The skills required for Level 5 are **b** good analysis and **c** good evaluation. **d** While the student evaluates each argument she makes throughout her answer, **e** there is one element missing in her evaluation. To reach the upper part of Level 5, the official AQA mark scheme required that a clear final judgement is made at the end of the answer. Providing the analysis and evaluation included in the rest of the answer are good, an 'over-arching' concluding paragraph that emphasises and brings together the main points made earlier in the answer is what separates a high Level 5 answer from a good Level 4 or low Level 5 answer. For example, she might have argued in her conclusion that within a particular country, 'I think that using subsidies would be the best of the three options because it can be focused on the poor.' She could then have argued that in the long run, the most effective and sustainable policies would include successful action against climate change (which reduces food production through contributing to desertification), research into better farming methods, and encouraging people to eat less meat.

Scored 45/50 = good grade A

Question 2 **The video game market**

Total for this question: 50 marks

Study Extracts A, B and C, and then answer all parts of the question which follow.

Extract A:

Actual and forecast of world sales of video game consoles, millions, 2006 to 2011

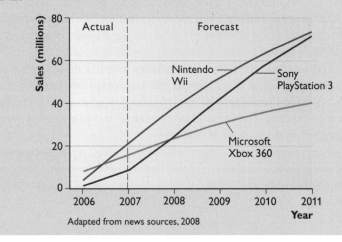

Adapted from news sources, 2008

Extract B:

Computer game war

In 2007, the Nintendo Wii became the fastest-selling game console in the world-wide video game market. But Nintendo admitted that sales had been held up by supply shortages, which led to excess demand for its product. The company under-estimated the growth of demand in the lead-up to the 2006 Christmas market, as the Wii became the 'must-have' game console, for both children and adult gamers. 5
Almost 200,000 Wii consoles were sold in the UK in December 2006, even though Nintendo launched the product in Europe only on 8 December.

Nintendo admitted demand for its Wii console, which has a motion-sensitive controller allowing users to mimic swinging a golf club or throwing a punch, brought supply shortages. It also suffered from alleged accidents in which the machine's 10
innovative controller had flown out of gamers' hands and smashed their television screens.

Microsoft, Sony and Nintendo are locked in a battle for the top spot in the £15.3bn industry's new console war. Microsoft claimed victory for its Xbox 360 games console in the key US holiday season, with Sony's PlayStation 3 being beaten into 15
third spot by Nintendo's Wii, as the next generation of game consoles begins to penetrate the market. The recent growth of Wii sales offsets the fact that Nintendo

had seen its share of the fixed-console market steadily decline since Sony introduced the PlayStation in the 1990s. However, Nintendo is now clawing back market share.

Adapted from news sources, 2008

Extract C:

Should games be banned or controlled?

Video games now dominate toy markets throughout the world, especially in high-income countries such as the USA and the UK. However, not everyone is happy with this dominance.

On the one hand, there are those, including many sports organisations, who claim that along with other social evils such as processed junk food, video games contribute 5 to growing health problems such as obesity and the early onset of diabetes.

On the other hand, there are those who believe that the sale of violent video games is a cause of social breakdown and gang-based crime, with more and more teenagers and young people becoming victims of gun and knife attacks. Some critics of video game culture insist the government should ban the sale of all games which involve 10 violence and sexual exploitation. Others go less far, demanding only the issue of PG certificates similar to those used for movies.

Adapted from news sources, 2008

---

[01]   **Define the term 'excess demand' (Extract B, line 3).**   (5 marks)

ⓔ As noted under Question 1, first part of a data-response question always asks for a definition of an economic term. Very often, as with this question, there are two words in the term you must define. To earn all 5 marks, your answer must address *both* the words in the term.

---

[02]   **Using Extract A, identify two significant points of comparison in the sales of the different video game consoles over the period shown.**   (8 marks)

ⓔ In recent exams, the second part of a data-response question has included the word 'significant'. If you compare insignificant points you won't earn any marks. It is always best to explain why your points of comparison are significant.

---

[03]   **With the help of an appropriate diagram, explain why, according to Extract B, shortages of the Nintendo Wii game console emerged in December 2006.**   (12 marks)

ⓔ It is quite common for the third part of a data-response question on a market to ask you to explain excess demand or excess supply. Since shortages imply excess demand, this is a disguised question on excess demand.

[04] **Do you agree that the sale of video games should be left to the free market and that governments should not intervene to ban or restrict their sale? Justify your answer.** (25 marks)

ⓔ The key instruction words in the final part of a data-response question are likely to be: 'Evaluate', 'Assess' or 'Do you agree?…Justify your answer'. All three are asking for evaluation — the first obviously so.

Student answer

[01] Excess demand occurs in a market when the price is below the equilibrium price and the amount of the good or service that consumers wish to buy is greater than the quantity of the good or service that firms are willing to supply. **a** Demand is the quantity of a good consumers want to buy at a particular price. **b** Shortages exist in the market whenever there is excess demand.

ⓔ **5/5 marks awarded.** This answer is precise and to the point and earns all five of the available marks. The answer defines both **a** excess demand and **b** demand.

[02] A first significant point of comparison **a** is the graph showing sales of all three games consoles growing or projected to grow through the whole data period. For example the Wii grows from zero at the beginning of 2006 to forecast sales of about 73 million at the end of 2011. A second significant point of comparison **a** is that Wii sales are above PlayStation 3 sales throughout the data period, and above Xbox 360 sales from mid-2006 onwards. **b**

ⓔ **4/8 marks awarded.** As was the case with the answer to the first data question on the rice market, this answer does not score full marks. Indeed it only earns half the available marks. **a** The points of comparison identified are significant, but **b** not enough statistical evidence is provided from the data to support these points, particularly the second point.

[03] Extract B identifies three factors **a** that were responsible for the shortage of Wii games consoles in December 2006. In the first place, Nintendo, the Japanese company that manufactures the console, had under-estimated demand. In my diagram below, estimated demand is shown by the dashed demand curve D_1, while the real position of the demand curve is shown by D_2. **b**

In the second place, there were supply-chain problems resulting from the launch of a completely new product. Technical problems meant that Nintendo could not increase supply of the newly introduced Wii in the busy market period before Christmas 2006. The supply curve S_1 is therefore positioned to the left in the diagram, and is very inelastic in the short term.

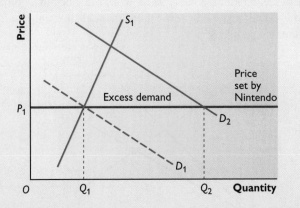

The third factor that led to the shortage was Nintendo under-pricing the Wii at P_1. In the diagram there would have been no shortage at this price had the demand curve been in the position Nintendo anticipated. However, with the demand curve in the position D_2, excess demand and shortages emerged at this price. The price would have had to be higher to get rid of the shortage.

ⓔ **12/12 marks awarded.** This is an excellent answer that fully merits all 12 marks. **a** The student rightly states that the Extract provides three prompts that suggest why shortages of Nintendo Wii consoles emerged. He develops all three prompts, though two would be enough for full marks — **b** providing of course that an accurate diagram is drawn, which the student does draw.

[04] With any good or service, production and consumption should be left to the free market if there is an absence of any significant market failure in the market. However, a case arises for some form of government intervention if market failure occurs, or if it is suspected that it will occur. Some forms of intervention, such as restrictions on sales, allow the market to exist but impose constraints on the way the market operates. Other forms of intervention, especially a ban, abolish the market or drive it underground into an illegal black market.

Although the data in the question does not use the term 'demerit good', the evidence provided in Extract C indicates that some video games, namely games that depict extreme violence, can be classified as demerit goods. **a** When demerit goods are consumed, negative externalities are discharged which harm the general public. Arguably, the people who play violent video games then display anti-social behaviour, which in extreme form results in their mimicking the video games and going out and hurting or killing complete strangers. A couple of years ago a 'moral panic' was stirred up by newspapers such as the *Sun* and the *Daily Express*, which blamed the spate of knife attacks and killings on London streets on video games.

But if a violent video game is a demerit good, as my diagram below shows, there may be a case for not banning them, but restricting their sale, from

Q_1 (the privately optimal level of sales) to Q_2 (the socially optimal level of sales). This could be done by restrictions on sales to children and to other impressionable people. **a**

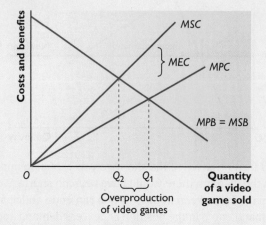

However, this may not be the best way forward. A policy option that would deal with the problem in a better way would be to censure the games by taking out their violent content. In effect, they would no longer be demerit goods. However, all these methods of intervention, bans, restrictions on sales and censorship may not work because they lead to problems of government failure. **b**

ⓔ **20/25 marks awarded.** This is a very good answer but not a perfect answer. It sits just above mid-Level 4, scoring 20 marks. **a** The answer is very strong on analysis, analysing the case for and against leaving the sale of video games to the free market. **a** The drawing and interpretation of the diagram depicting a violent video game as a demerit good also shows analytical skill. The answer is weaker in terms of the main skill required in a part [04] answer, evaluation. After an excellent introduction which sets the scene for a very good answer, the student analyses well the issues posed by the question. However, the student is less good at evaluating in any depth the different policies government might use to deal with the problem posed by violent games. He does not query whether most video games are violent or non-violent. **b** The possibility of government failure replacing market failure is brought in at the end of the answer, but left limply hanging in the air. A stronger concluding paragraph is needed to reach Level 5.

Scored 41/50 = grade A

Question 3 **Economies of scale and the division of labour**

Total for this question: 50 marks

Study Extracts A, B and C, and then answer all parts of the question which follow.

Extract A:

Economies and diseconomies of scale in container transport

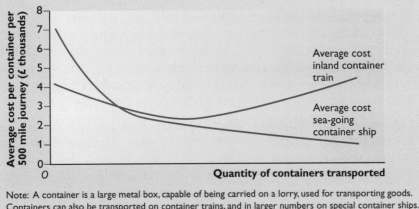

Note: A container is a large metal box, capable of being carried on a lorry, used for transporting goods. Containers can also be transported on container trains, and in larger numbers on special container ships. Containers now carry a significant fraction of goods moved between countries and inside countries.

Adapted from news sources, 2008

Extract B:

Economies of scale and the mass production of cars

Since the development of the Model T Ford car in the first decade of the twentieth century, economies of scale have been of great importance in the automobile industry. However, while diseconomies of scale seldom occur in the car industry, globalisation (the increasing integration of national economies throughout the world) is making most car manufacturers vulnerable to competition from rivals 5 in other countries who also benefit from economies of scale. In today's global car industry, a mass-producing car company must produce millions of vehicles a year, or face going out of business.

In 2005, the 30 or so leading global car manufacturers divided into two categories, with about 15 firms in each category. Each of the members of the top category 10 produced millions of cars a year and enjoyed substantial economies of scale.

By contrast, each of the firms in the lower division produced less than a million cars a year. Lacking economies of scale, the smaller mass-producing companies were below the productively efficient size and suffering a significant cost disadvantage when compared with their larger rivals. Before it went out of business in 2005, the 15 UK's MG Rover Group was in the lower division of leading world mass producers.

Its relatively small size meant Rover could not compete with industry giants such as Toyota.

Adapted from news sources, 2008

Extract C:

Car production and the division of labour

Division of labour is one of the hallmarks of a modern economy, contributing to productive efficiency and increased productivity. In the early twentieth century, Ford's assembly-line production provided the perfect example of how the division of labour leads to increased labour productivity.

Prior to Henry Ford's introduction of the assembly line, cars were produced by 5 craftsmen, as was the case with most manufactured goods. Each car was individually produced by a team of skilled workers. In order to build a car, craftsmen had to be highly skilled and knowledgeable about automobile technology. Every person on the team possessed a very good working knowledge of virtually every aspect of car manufacture. Many craftsmen were capable of building an entire car by themselves. 10

Then Ford came along and started to build cars using the assembly line process. With the assembly line, a small team of specialists designed the car and assembly process, and a larger team of generally unskilled workers built the cars. Workers, or indeed anybody taken off the street, no longer had to know much or anything about cars. They could work on the wheel assembly section without having ever seen a car 15 engine in their lives. The process was faster, cheaper and more efficient than craft production.

With the division of labour, the individual needs only to know how to do his or her specific task and nothing more. The assembly-line worker requires no large-scale knowledge, no vision nor any concept of the whole. As long as workers can turn the 20 screw when a piece is in front of them, that's all they need to know and do.

Adapted from news sources, 2008

[01]   Define the term 'diseconomies of scale' (Extract B, line 3).   (5 marks)

🄔 For this part [01] question, the mark scheme would be presented as follows.
For an acceptable definition such as:
- 'Increasing average costs as the size of a firm increases'; or 'Rising unit costs as the scale at which a firm operates increases'   **5 marks**

If the definition is incomplete or inaccurate, marks may be broken down as follows:
- Stating that a diseconomy of scale is the opposite of an economy of scale.   **I mark**

[02]   Using Extract A, identify two significant points of comparison between the economies and diseconomies of scale experienced by a container ship and those experienced by a container train.   (8 marks)

e In this case, the graph shows only a limited number of points of comparison. When selecting your comparative points, you must indicate why you consider them to be significant.

---

[03]   '...the division of labour leads to increased labour productivity' (Extract C, lines 3–4). Using an example *other* than one relating to the car industry, explain how the division of labour increases labour productivity.   (12 marks)

e The key instruction in a part [03] question is to *explain*. This requires the skill of *analysis*, which earns 24% of the total marks available for the ECON 1 examination. Analysis marks are earned in the part [03] answer, and also in the lead-up to evaluation in the part [04] answer.

---

[04]   Do you agree that economies of scale always lead to monopoly *and* that monopolies caused by economies of scale are generally good for the economy? Justify your answer.   (25 marks)

e Quite often, as in this case, a part [04] question contains a weasel word such as 'always'. Whenever you see this word in the question (or similar words such as 'must', 'inevitably' and 'solely'), you should recognise that if you agree 100% with the central assertion in the question, your mark is likely to be quite low. The same is true if you 100% disagree. The best way to answer the question is to take an 'it all depends on circumstances, or on the assumptions I am making' approach to the answer.

Student answer

[01]   A diseconomy of scale is the opposite of an economy of scale. **a** With an economy of scale a firm's total costs fall as output increases. By contrast with a diseconomy of scale, total costs rise as output increases. **b**

e **1/5 marks awarded.** This answer is wrong. Economies and diseconomies of scale are defined in terms of average costs and not total costs **b**. But while the mark scheme for a part [01] question allows full marks to be awarded for a short, sharp, accurate answer, it also provides an avenue for fewer marks to be awarded for relevant points even though, taken together, they don't add up to a correct answer. So in this case, **a** 1 mark is earned, for stating that diseconomies of scale are the opposite of economies of scale. Part [01] mark schemes are sometimes thought to be deliberately generous to students, maybe because a purpose of the first part of the question is to ease you into the more demanding and difficult later parts of the question.

[02]   Economies and diseconomies of scale can be shown by the shape of a firm's average cost curve. In the case of a 'U'-shaped average cost curve (inland container trains), economies of scale are benefited from moving along the downward-sloping section of the average cost curve, from £7,000 a container for a 500 mile journey when presumably only one container is carried on a container train, to about £3,000 a container when the optimal number of containers are on the train. After that point, average costs rise again (diseconomies of scale), reaching about £4,500 per container at the right-hand end of the 'U'-shaped curve. By contrast, the average cost curve for sea-going container ships is downward-sloping throughout its length, indicating economies of scale only. **a**

Also, the two average cost curves intersect at about £3,200 per container. At this quantity of containers carried, container trains and container ships have no advantage or disadvantage against each other.

ⓔ 8/8 marks awarded. Although this answer is not organised as well as it could be, it does enough to earn all 8 marks. **a** Average costs are compared for container trains with regard to both economies and diseconomies of scale, and the data are used to support the points made. Although the data are not used to support the point about container ships experiencing economies of scale but not diseconomies of scale, the last paragraph makes a further comparison and supports the point from the data. Finally, it is worth noting, that despite the incorrect definitions provided in the answer to part [01], diseconomies of scale are accurately defined here. Unfortunately marks cannot be carried across to boost the mark for part [01].

[03] Division of labour means different workers specialising in different tasks. Labour productivity is output per worker. **a** The example I shall provide to illustrate the division of labour increasing labour productivity occurred at my school. As in all secondary schools, my school employs specialist teachers to teach different subjects. My economics teacher is an excellent teacher who has improved her teaching over the years by becoming more knowledgeable about the subject. Thus, although it is difficult to measure output per worker in service industries such as education, her output measured in exam passes and grades is high.

However, in February, my economics teacher was ill for a few weeks. The business studies teacher in my school took on some extra lessons and taught us. Although he tried hard, he was not used to the subject and was not as productive as the economics teacher had been. My economics teacher says that economics teachers can teach business studies but that business studies teachers find it difficult to teach economics. As my experience shows, this may well be the case. However, business studies teachers will probably disagree! **b**

ⓔ 12/12 marks awarded. This is a nice home-spun answer that does enough for full marks. **a** The student starts the answer by providing accurate definitions of the two key concepts in the question. It is always a good idea to do this. Marks can be earned from accurate definition, and the definitions provide a platform for launching the rest of the answer without drifting into irrelevance. **b** The second paragraph is irrelevant, but by this time, full marks have already been earned.

[04] In the case of natural monopoly, economies of scale do lead to monopoly. This follows from the definition of a natural monopoly, which is a market or industry in which there is only room in the market for one firm benefiting to the full from economies of scale. Such a situation is illustrated in the diagram below. **a**

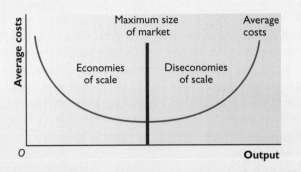

However, if we remove the market size constraint, there can be room in the market for more than one firm benefiting to the full from economies of scale. A good example is provided by the car industry in Extracts B and C. **b** In conclusion, economies of scale can justify monopoly but economies of scale don't always lead to monopoly. It is also worth noting that when there is only one firm in an industry in a country, there appears to be a monopoly. However, if the market is open to international trade, competition from imports may considerably reduce the monopoly power of the so-called monopoly.

Monopolies are generally good for the economy if the lower average costs created by economies of scale are passed on to consumers in the form of lower prices. Such monopolies can also be good for the economy if the monopolies use their profits to finance research and development (R&D) of new products and more productively efficient ways of making existing products.

However, even when a monopoly is formed as a result of the 'virtuous' pursuit of economies of scale, there is always the danger that, once formed, the monopoly could use its market power to exploit consumers. It might restrict output and hike up the price; it may refuse to innovate, and it may also restrict consumer choice. **c**

For this reason, governments often regulate monopolies to try to make sure that they continue to behave in a virtuous way and are not tempted to slip into monopoly abuse. But if regulation is non-existent or ineffective (an example of government failure), monopoly may not generally be good for the economy, even when substantial economies of scale are enjoyed by the monopoly. A recent case has been the British Airport Authority which used to have monopoly control over the three main London airports. Although BAA benefits from substantial economies of scale, it was criticised for exploiting passengers, for example by creating too many luxury stores at the airports it owns, at the expense of customer toilets and seats for passengers waiting to fly. **d**

In conclusion, my answer to both parts of the question is that economies of scale don't always lead to monopoly, but when they do, whether the monopoly is good for the economy depends on the monopoly's behaviour or conduct, and on whether effective regulatory constraints are in place to force the monopoly to behave itself.

ⓔ **24/25 marks awarded.** This is an excellent answer that certainly reaches Level 4 in the generic AQA mark scheme for part [04] questions. In fact, because of the good evaluation and reasonable conclusion shown in the answer, it is placed at the mid-point of Level 5, almost earning full marks. The slightly limp conclusion explains why full marks have not been awarded.

a The student uses the case of natural monopoly to show how economies of scale can lead to monopoly. **b** He then uses the prompt provided by the car industry in Extracts B and C when arguing that large size does not inevitably lead to monopoly. **c** He continues by arguing that a monopoly may behave virtuously, but the danger that it will start to abuse its power justifies regulation. **d** A second example (BAA) is then chosen from his general knowledge. Throughout his answer he analyses and evaluates.

Scored 45/50 = good grade A

Question 4 **The price of oil and the US car market**

Total for this question: 50 marks

Study Extracts A, B and C, and then answer all parts of the question which follow.

Extract A:

Sales of small, medium-size and large cars in the USA, January to May 2008, as a percentage of total vehicle sales, including trucks

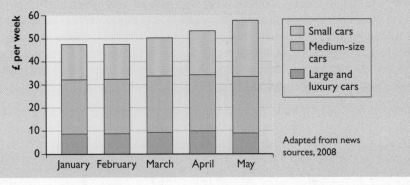

Adapted from news sources, 2008

Extract B:

Why the price of oil must rise

If oil were like most other products, its high price might not matter very much. There would be little reason for the US government to worry about people's driving habits. But oil is different, for two main reasons.

First, oil is a scarce resource that is disproportionately controlled by unfriendly foreign governments. Second, the use of oil produces negative externalities, namely emissions of CO_2, which are heating up the planet and which will eventually cause all sorts of problems. The planet's 10 warmest years on record have all occurred since 1995. It seems pretty clear that we'd be better off if we could figure out how to use less oil. 　　　　5

So the US Senate is deciding whether to introduce a 'permits to pollute' scheme to try to reduce carbon emissions. These changes would of course make energy use more expensive. However, the only reliable way to cut oil use is to make oil more 　10 expensive. Yet opponents of the proposed new carbon rules argue that oil costs way too much already. But that argument gets cause and effect almost perfectly backward. Oil has become so expensive mainly because the world is using so much of it. Yes, making it more expensive — about 40 cents a gallon more expensive by 2030, according to two analyses of the current cap and trade bill — will bring some 　15 medium-term economic pain. But the pain can be greatly reduced through broad-based tax cuts on income and on other goods, financed with the revenue raised by the 'permits to pollute' scheme (or, as many economists prefer, a carbon tax).

20

As unpleasant as it has been, the increase in petrol prices has brought one big advantage. It has shown how flexible American consumers are — how well they can adapt to new prices, for example by buying smaller cars, without turning their lives upside down.

Adapted from news sources, 2008

Extract C:

A structural change in the US car market?

Americans fell in love with vehicles like Ford pick-up trucks in the 1990s, back when petrol prices were stable at around $1 a gallon. But this stability was actually a sign of something deeply unusual. The cost of almost everything else was rising, as was the size of people's nominal pay checks. So in practical terms, petrol was becoming cheaper. By 1999, it had effectively fallen to its lowest point on record, about 30% 5 lower than in the 1950s and '60s.

Cheap petrol made a large pick-up truck a highly desirable luxury shopping item. The recent increase in petrol prices to $3.98 a gallon has changed that. While a large pick-up truck costs $100,000 to drive over five years, a Ford Focus costs less than $40,000 — a difference of $60,000. The annual pre-tax income of a typical American 10 family is also about $60,000. So choosing the pick-up truck over a Focus is like volunteering for a 20% pay cut.

No wonder, then, that Americans are changing their driving habits so quickly. With sales plummeting, General Motors (GM) has just said that it would stop making pick-up trucks and sport utility vehicles at four of its North American plants. Rick 15 Wagoner, GM's chairman, thinks that the shift toward more fuel-efficient cars is a sign of a permanent structural change in the US car market.

The unyielding reality is that price matters, enormously. That's all you need to know about the car market these days. And it's almost all you need to know about the debate over energy policy. 20

Adapted from news sources, 2008

---

[01] **Define the term 'scarce resource' (Extract B, line 4).** (5 marks)

e To earn all 5 of the available marks, you must address both words in the term in the question: namely, 'scarce' and 'resource'.

---

[02] **With the help of Extract A, identify two significant features of the changes in new vehicle sales in the USA over the period shown.** (8 marks)

e This is an example of a question which asks for identification of two significant *features* of the data rather than for a *comparison* of two separate data series. Part [02] questions are generally worded in this way when the graph or table in the question contains only one data series. (The data in this question are actually more complicated as the bars in the bar graph are disaggregated into the sub-categories of small, medium-sized and large cars.) By contrast, if two data series are in the data, students are generally asked to identify two significant points of comparison.

[03] **Extract B (lines 10–11) mentions that the US government may introduce a 'permits to pollute' scheme to reduce carbon emissions. Explain how a 'permits to pollute' scheme operates.**   (12 marks)

ⓔ Usually part [03] of a question on a market instructs you to draw an 'appropriate diagram' as part of your answer. However, as this question shows, this is not always the case. It is difficult to think of a diagram that could help explain how the 'permits to pollute' system operates!

Whether or not a diagram is required, to score maximum marks for a written explanation, your answer must contain logical links in a chain of reasoning. For this question, the linkages in a logical chain of reasoning (shown here with the mark scheme) might be:

A 'permit to pollute' is an upper-limit regulation **(2 marks)**; which is tradable between polluters **(2 marks)**; polluters who reduce pollution by more than the law requires sell their spare permits **(2 marks)** to polluters unable to reduce pollution by the required amount **(2 marks)**; incentives are created for polluters to reduce pollution **(2 marks)**; each year the upper limit for pollution may be reduced **(2 marks)** creating further incentives for pollution reduction **(up to 10 marks in total)**.

[04] **In 2008 motorists in the UK and the USA put pressure on their governments to reduce rather than to increase the price of petrol. Evaluate the case for and against reducing the price of petrol: for example, through lower taxation on fuels.**   (25 marks)

ⓔ It is important to familiarise yourself with the skills needed to reach the higher levels in the mark scheme. Reaching the higher levels usually guarantees a grade A across the paper as a whole (though you have to do well in the objective test section of the paper, and in the earlier parts of the data question). To reach Level 4 or Level 5, you don't have to display all the skills listed in the mark scheme. However, you must certainly display most of the listed skills. Level 4 requires good analysis and limited evaluation, but Level 5 requires both good analysis and good evaluation.

Student answer

[01] A resource is an input into the production process. **a** Natural resources include fertile soils and mineral and energy deposits. Man-made resources include capital equipment and skilled workers (human capital). All these resources are scarce if costs of production are involved. **b** In this situation, the price mechanism may ration the scarce resources. But if price is too low, or if the good is provided at zero price, resources will be scarce in relation to demand.

ⓔ **5/5 marks awarded.** The answer is sufficiently accurate and shows sufficient understanding of both words (**a** resource and **b** scarce) so picks up all 5 available marks. There is some 'benefit of the doubt' involved in awarding these, but on balance, the student has done just enough to earn full marks.

[02] A first significant feature of the data is that total car sales grew as a percentage of total vehicle sales over the five month period from about 47% in January 2008 to about 48% in May 2008. **a**

A second significant feature is that sales of large and luxury cars remained more or less flat at around 9% of total vehicle sales over all five months, whereas sales of small cars grew after February (having been flat at around 15% of total vehicle sales in January and February) to around 26% in May.

ⓔ **8/8 marks awarded.** Again, full marks are earned. The answer does all that is required by the mark scheme: namely, to identify two significant features of the changes in new vehicle sales, backed up with statistical evidence drawn from Extract A. **a** It is worth noting that because it is difficult for a student in the exam room to read accurately the numbers on a small graph, examiners are given a certain amount of latitude when granting marks for statistical evidence. For example, in this case the student would have earned the same marks for stating that total vehicle sales grew from about 46% to about 49% over the period. However, numbers that lie outside this range would be deemed to be insufficiently accurate to merit reward.

[03] A permits to pollute (or emission trading) scheme involves a mix of 'command and control' regulation and market forces. Command and control regulation takes the form of the government or a regulatory agency set up by government imposing a maximum emission limit on pollution, which may be reduced year-by-year in the years following the establishment of the permits to pollute system. Market forces operate in the sense that the polluting firms that are subject to the scheme have an incentive to reduce pollution each year by more than the law requires, in order to make money by selling their 'spare' pollution permits to other firms that decide not to, or cannot, reduce pollution by the required amount each year. The polluting firms that buy the 'spare' pollution permits remain within the law even though they are exceeding the pollution limit. However, purchasing pollution permits raises their costs of production, so they have an incentive to 'get their act together' by adopting clean technologies and/or energy sources that will allow them in future years to reduce pollution by the required amount. **a**

In theory, a permits to pollute system is a 'win-win-win' solution to the problem that results from pollution. The first winners are the firms that make money out of reducing pollution by more than the required amount each year. The second winners are the firms that fail to reduce pollution in this way, but which can still comply with the law by purchasing 'spare' pollution permits. Finally, the third winners are the governments that create the market in permits to pollute, because (in theory) it is a successful market-orientated way of reducing the emission of negative externalities.

ⓔ **12/12 marks awarded.** Again, this is an excellent answer that fully deserves all 12 marks. **a** The answer displays a sound understanding of a 'permits to pollute' emissions trading system. However, for a part [03] question, the answer is a little over-long. Although the student goes on to write an excellent part [04] answer, over-long answers to part [03] questions often result in students running out of time on part [04] where evaluation skills have to be shown.

[04] It is sometimes said, usually by members of the general public rather than by economists, that a significant rise in the price of a good is evidence of market failure and a factor that contributes to inflation getting out of control.

However, rising (and falling) relative prices of one good in terms of other goods are all part of the way a market economy operates. If the supply of a good becomes scarce, relative to the demand for the good, its price should rise to get rid of the excess demand that would otherwise persist in the market.

Recently, the price of oil has increased relative to the price of other goods because of an increase in demand, caused in part by growing demand from 'emerging market' countries, especially the so-called 'BRIC' countries (Brazil, Russia, India and China). On the one hand, a higher relative price may indicate that producing oil is a very profitable activity. If this happens, oil production increases in response to the demand stimulus. But on the other hand, the higher relative price may cause some users of oil to substitute other sources of energy in place of oil. The information signalled by changing relative prices thus creates incentives for producers and consumers to alter market behaviour in a way that contributes eventually to a more efficient allocation of resources.

The logic of the above argument is that governments, including the UK government, should not intervene in the market for oil to try to reduce its price. Everything should be left to Adam Smith's 'invisible hand' of the market. **a** After all, economics is about economising, and a higher price of oil creates the incentive both for consumers to economise and for industries such as the automobile industry to develop new technologies which either don't use oil or which are more fuel (oil) efficient.

But as the response in 2008 of the UK government to the rise in the price of oil to above $140 a barrel indicates, governments often react to other pressures. First and foremost, they are scared of losing votes and of being kicked out of office at the next general election. The pressure of motoring organisations and truck drivers who squeal that motorists are being crucified by rising fuel prices leads to governments going soft on or indeed abandoning previous commitments to preserving both the environment and sustainable resources. This is despite the fact that, for many years before the recent rise in the price of oil, the cost of motoring had fallen significantly in real terms, and the considerable evidence that the falling real cost of motoring had led to the purchase of huge gas-guzzling '4 x 4s' by people who previously had never been able to afford them. **b**

Nevertheless, there may be a case for governments to take temporary action, which will later be reversed, to slow down the rate at which the prices of petrol and diesel fuels rise. This is because rapid price increases act as an 'outside supply shock' which destabilises the economy and produces victims such as rural motorists who have to drive long distances each day. However, such intervention by governments should indeed be only temporary and must not get in the way of market forces producing the necessary adjustments to the fact that scarce oil resources are fast running out.

ⓔ **20/25 marks awarded.** This is an interesting and thoughtful answer. **a** The first part of the answer is particularly strong, since it sets out extremely well the case for governments not intervening in the market and as the writer says, leaving things to Adam Smith's 'invisible hand'.

b However, the second half of the essay lapses somewhat into what examiners call a 'general studies' answer, which is strong on opinion and a 'man-in-the-street' approach to important issues, but somewhat devoid of the analytical precision needed as a bedrock for the rigorous evaluation that should follow. The student could have provided this analysis by making use of the prompt in the question to consider the effect of lower taxation on the price of fuel. More discussion is also needed on the potential conflict between protecting vulnerable groups of motorists on the one hand and maintaining the government's commitment to meet its environmental objectives on the other hand.

The first half of the answer earns a low Level 4 mark, but the 'general studies' approach of the second half means that a Level 5 mark is not awarded.

Scored 45/50 = good grade A

Question 5 **Lads' mags and demerit goods**

Total for this question: 50 marks

Study Extracts A, B and C, and then answer all parts of the question which follow.

Extract A:

Sales of 'lads' mags' and other men's magazines, 2006 and 2007

Lads' mags	Sales: June to December 2007	Percentage change in sales over previous year
Nuts	277,269	−9.0%
Zoo	188,732	−18.1%
FHM	311,590	−25.9%
Loaded	120,492	−35.0%
Other men's magazines		
GQ	127,886	+ 0.9%
Esquire	53,537	+ 2.1%
Men's Health	235,833	+ 2.1%

Adapted from news sources

Extract B:

Is a lads' mag a demerit good?

Lads' mags contain many erotic images and advertisements, but their publishers do not consider them to be pornographic. Despite the fact that a lads' mag may be deemed to be a demerit good, the magazines are often prominently displayed in newsagents' shops, with no restrictions on whether they can be located next to comics and children's sweets. Indeed, lads' mags can be sold to all age groups,   5
children included. However, some people argue that lads' mags should be regulated or taxed so as to reduce their availability and sales.

Lads' mags are at the forefront of a wider move towards the normalisation of pornography, by rebranding pornographic images as 'not porn' but 'sexy images of glamour models'. Indeed, publishers claim that the sale of lads' mags empowers   10
women and adds to their aspirations. However, the real truth is that the perpetual representation of women as sex objects is extremely dangerous and demeaning.

Adapted from news sources, 2008

Extract C:

Sex doesn't sell as lads' mags suffer

The success of magazines, such as *Loaded* and *FHM*, which target young men with a menu of sex, sport, gadgets and grooming tips, was one of the publishing phenomena of the 1990s. However, in recent years the sales of these magazines have fallen. The internet is believed to be responsible for the drop in sales as more and more men go to the web to view scantily clad women. 5

Loaded, founded in 1994, came to symbolise the genre and attracted a wide readership through its tongue-in-cheek journalism and ability to persuade celebrities to dispense with most of their clothes for photo shoots. But as sales dropped, many critics accused men's magazines of increasingly dumbing down and resorting to greater levels of nudity in a bid to halt the slide. 10

However, the up-market men's glossy sector fared rather better. *GQ*, published by Conde Nast and which does not sell on sex, sold an average of 129,520 in the second half of 2007, gaining 2,000 readers year on year. *Esquire*, which has been relaunched in 'manbag' size, is one of the few men's titles to have recorded a slight increase in circulation — up 2.1% to 53,537. 15

Among men's titles selling more than 100,000 copies, the biggest winner was fitness title *Men's Health*, which rose 3.4% year on year to 235,833, with *GQ*, also up 0.9% year on year to 127,886. *Men's Health* has now leapfrogged *Zoo* to become the third-highest-selling men's magazine.

Adapted from news sources

---

[01]   Define the term 'demerit good' (Extract B, line 3).   (5 marks)

(e) Many exam questions on goods such as tobacco and alcohol avoid stating that the good might be deemed to be a demerit good. It is up to you, the student, to judge whether or not the good is a demerit good and then to include relevant analysis of demerit goods in your answers to parts [03] and [04]. However, in this case, because the question asks for a definition, the term 'demerit good' does figure in the wording of the question. Make sure you avoid the temptation to classify all goods as being either merit goods or demerit goods. You will earn no marks for such an approach.

---

[02]   Using Extract A, identify two significant points of comparison in the changing sales of men's magazines over the period shown.   (8 marks)

(e) When answering part [02] of a data-response question and quoting statistics to support your points of comparison, you must always state the units in which the data are presented. For this question, the numbers are shown as percentages, so a % sign is needed for each number quoted. For other questions, the units of measurement may take a variety of forms. Prices measured in pounds or dollars, quantity units such as kilos or tonnes, and data presented in index number form have all appeared in past examinations.

[03]   '...some people argue that lads' mags should be regulated or taxed so as to reduce their availability and sales' (Extract B, lines 6–7).

With the use of an appropriate diagram, explain how a sales tax might affect the market for lads' mags.   (12 marks)

@ Besides usually requiring the drawing of an appropriate diagram, part [03] questions test the skill of analysis. This requires selecting relevant information from the data source(s) and then using the information, perhaps as evidence, in the answer. Information in the data is there to provide a prompt for your answer. You should indicate which bits of the data you are using but avoid just 'copying out' sentences or numbers from the data.

[04]   **Discuss whether governments can and should attempt to control the publication of photographs which exploit women, in lads' mags and on the internet. Make sure you include economic arguments in your answer.**   (25 marks)

@ As previously stated, evaluation is the main skill tested in part [04] questions. Competing theories or explanations often lead into evaluation. Explaining why, in your view, some arguments or lines of reasoning are more important than others is also a route to good evaluation. Where appropriate, you should weigh up alternative and competing theories. Likewise, you must state and consider the assumptions you are making.

Student answer

[01]   A demerit good can be defined as any good that is socially bad for the community as a whole. **a** Examples include tobacco and alcohol. **b**

@ **3/5 marks awarded.** Although the answer is about the right length for a part [01] question, it earns only 2 of the 5 marks available. Full marks could be earned by defining a demerit good, either in terms of the negative externalities suffered by the wider population when a person consumes a demerit good, or in terms of over-consumption because consumers ignore the long-term private costs they will eventually incur. Either way, through the externalities or the information problem route, resource misallocation occurs. The outcome is then less than socially optimal. **a** However, in the case of this answer, it is insufficient to define a demerit good simply as being 'socially bad'. This part of the answer picks up 2 marks, **b** to which a third mark is added for providing an example.

[02]   The main change in the magazine sales shown in Extract A, a change which is also described in Extract C, is the fall in sales of so-called 'lads' mags' and the growth in sales of 'other men's' magazines. *FHM*, the lads' mag with the highest sales, dropped by 25.9 between the second half of 2006 and the second quarter of 2007, while the sales of *Men's Health*, the 'other magazine' with the biggest sales, increased by 2.1. **a**

   This was also the largest percentage increase (although sales of *Esquire* grew by a similar percentage, albeit from an initial lower total of sales).

   Among the lads' mags, by contrast, *Loaded* suffered the largest percentage fall in sales, by 35.

ⓔ **6/8 marks awarded.** While the student makes two significant points of comparison, **a** unfortunately he misses out some of the units of measurement. The data are measured as percentages. Failing to state the units of measurement means that, for each point of comparison, I mark is automatically docked.

[03] A sales tax is a tax imposed on the firms which sell the taxed good. In the UK, there are two kinds of sales tax. The first is an ad valorem tax (such as VAT), which is currently levied at 20.0% of the price of the good without the tax. The second type of tax is a specific tax or unit tax, in which the size of the tax is not related to the price of the good without the tax. Specific taxes on goods such as alcohol and tobacco are levied at very high rates to discourage consumption of the goods. **a** If lads' mags are judged by the government to be demerit goods, with similar properties to cigarettes or alcohol, the government might decide to levy a high specific tax on these magazines. The possible effect of such a tax is illustrated in the diagrams below.

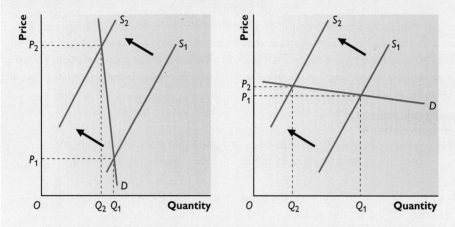

In both diagrams, the tax is very high, which shifts the supply curve of lads' mags significantly to the left or upward. However, in the left-hand diagram, I have assumed that the demand curve for lads' mags is almost completely price inelastic (because men are addicted to the product on offer). This assumption means that the rise in price is proportionately much greater than the fall in sales. By contrast, the right-hand diagram assumes that the demand for lads' mags is highly price elastic. Given this assumption, a high tax imposed on lads' mags leads to a much greater percentage fall in their sales. By contrast, if 20% VAT is imposed on lads' mags (currently they are zero rated for VAT), it will have relatively little absolute effect on sales, even if demand is elastic, because the price won't rise by very much.

ⓔ **12/12 marks awarded.** This answer is excellent and earns the maximum mark of 12. Indeed by including and explaining two diagrams (instead of the one required by the question), together with a lot of detail about the UK system of indirect taxation, the answer goes further than is required to earn full marks. **a** Once again, the danger here lies in over-writing the answer to part [03] and not having enough time to develop the following answer to part [04], which carries 25 marks as against the 12 available for part [03].

AQA AS Economics

[04] The main argument for the government controlling publication of magazines which include photographs which exploit and abuse women stems from the assumption that such magazines are significant examples of demerit goods. Arguably the publication of such photographs exploits and degrades both the women involved and women in general, and it might also lead to anti-social behaviour directed against women by the men who look at the pictures.

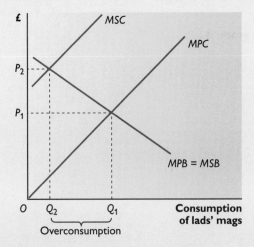

The diagram above illustrates how lads' mags may be analysed as a demerit good. **a** The social costs to the whole community resulting from the consumption of lads' mags exceed the private costs incurred by the consumer. The private cost can be measured by the money cost of purchasing the magazine, together with any health damage suffered by the reader. However, the social costs of consumption include the costs of damage and injury inflicted on other people, particularly women. **b**

As my diagram illustrates, in the absence of taxation, too many lads' mags are bought at a market price P_1. At least in the short term, the privately optimal level of consumption is Q_1, where $MPB = MPC$. This is greater than the socially optimal level of consumption, Q_2, located where $MSB = MSC$. Provided the various cost and benefit curves are in the positions in which I have located them in my diagram, there is a case for imposing a tax on lads' mags to take their price up to P_2. However, if I had positioned the MSC curve considerably to the left of where I have drawn it in the diagram, the socially optimal level of consumption would be zero. If this were so, there would be a case for banning lads' mags, or at least for censoring their content. Conversely, if we argue that lads' mags are completely harmless, both for the reader and also for the women whose photographs appear in the magazines, there would be a case for doing nothing at all and for allowing people their freedoms. I tend to be a libertarian rather than an authoritarian, so this is very much in line with my own views.

ⓔ **14/25 marks awarded. b** The student obeys the instruction in the question to include economic arguments in his answer and **a** applies the standard analysis of demerit goods to the case study in the question: namely, lads' mags. To earn a higher Level 4 mark (this answer has been placed just above the mid-point of Level 3), a slightly wider answer is needed: for example, developing further the case for and against different types of intervention, and discussing the possibility that intervention will lead to government failure, for example through the emergence of a black market in lads' mags smuggled into the country. Picking up a prompt in the data, it could also be argued that controlling lads' mags is much less important than trying to abolish the much more offensive material that can be accessed on the internet. The key words in the question are *can* and *should*. The answer needs to give more emphasis to these words if Level 4 is to be reached.

Scored 35/50 = good grade B

Question 6 **Merit goods, private goods and public goods**

Total for this question: 50 marks

Study Extracts A, B and C, and then answer all parts of the question which follow.

Extract A:

Numbers of pupils in independent and state schools in the UK, selected years 1998 to 2007

Year	Number of pupils in independent schools	Number of pupils in state schools	Total pupils*
1998	556,230	7,533,470	8,260,580
2000	560,560	7,617,160	8,345,820
2002	578,580	7,627,430	8,369,080
2004	586,940	7,577,490	8,334,880
2006	580,510	7,455,730	8,215,690
2007	577,670	7,376,170	8,149,180

*Note: totals do not add up because certain categories of school, such as special needs schools, are missing from the table.

Source: Office for National Statistics

Extract B:

Education: private good, merit good or public good?

The education provided by private schools (or independent schools) is a form of private good. As with all private goods, buyers and sellers meet through the price mechanism. If they agree on a price, the ownership or use of the good (or service) can be transferred. Thus private goods tend to be excludable. They have clearly identified owners; and they tend to be rival.   5

But many economists believe that education is better regarded as a merit good that is under-produced and under-consumed if provision is left solely to the price mechanism. For this reason, governments often provide education completely free or they make use of subsidies. Either way, taxpayers pick up the bill, either directly for state provision of education, or indirectly by subsidising children attending private 10 schools.

For the most part, education is both a private good and a merit good. However, technical progress means that some forms of education have become public goods. Universities are placing their courses online and making them freely available to all. These courses can be 'consumed' by an unlimited number of students.

Technology-borne education is non-rivalrous and can be replicated and disseminated virtually cost-free to the next consumer through the internet, radio and television. Nevertheless, in principle, it is possible to exclude free-riders from all forms of education. It is perfectly possible to exclude students from access to education, both online and offline, if the education provider so wishes. In the UK, web-based 'tutor2u' provides some economics resources and courses free, but also charges teachers and students for other resources: for example, those accessed via the tutor2u virtual learning environment (VLE).

15

20

Adapted from news sources, 2008

Extract C:

The battle between Independent and state schools

Chris Parry, the chief executive of the Independent Schools Council, has launched a stinging attack on the 'very poor' quality of state education in Britain. Mr Parry believes that the quality of education provided in state schools is 'offensive' to parents who pay their taxes, and forces hundreds of thousands to go private.

Mr Parry said: 'I find it very offensive that I can't find provision in the maintained sector for my child... Where I come from the maintained sector is very poor and my wife and I have made sacrifices to send both our children to the independent sector.

5

'There are thousands of families like mine who have chosen to make that commitment both to their child's future and to the future of this country — and at significant expense, I might add.'

10

However, Francis Green, professor of economics at Kent University, said independent schools were not doing enough to justify the tax breaks they enjoy from the fact that the government allows them to operate as charities. He said 'Charities are supposed to help the general public, but most private schools provide only limited public benefit.'

15

Adapted from news sources, 2008

[01] **Define the term 'subsidies' (Extract B, line 9).** (5 marks)

(e) A surprisingly large proportion of AS economics students don't understand the meaning of the term 'subsidies'. Comically, many confuse subsidies with 'subsidence'. An example of subsidence is the slippage of land beneath a building and the term has nothing to do with giving money to firms.

[02]   Using Extract A, identify two significant points of comparison between the number of pupils in the UK attending independent and state schools over the period shown.   (8 marks)

Ⓔ Extract A in this question shows absolute totals for pupils attending private and state schools, e.g. 7,533,470 attending state schools in 1998. Rather than quoting large numbers like this one in your answer, you might decide to convert the number into a percentage of total pupils. For example, your answer could compare state school attendance as a proportion of total pupils peaking at 91.3% in 2000, as against independent school attendance peaking at 7.1% of the total in 2006. Make sure you take a calculator into the exam room so you can perform such calculations.

[03]   With the use of an appropriate diagram, explain why too little education may be provided if the service is only available through the market.   (12 marks)

Ⓔ The part of the mark scheme which the examiner will use to award marks for a diagram on a merit good will look something like this:

Labelling the vertical axis 'Costs/benefits' (also accept 'Costs', 'Benefits', '£s') and the horizontal axis 'Quantity of education' (also accept 'Quantity'), initial positions of the MPC, MSC, MPB and MSB curves	1 mark
Drawing the MSC line to the right of the MPC line	1 mark
Vertical co-ordinate drawn and labelled where MPB = MPC	1 mark
Vertical co-ordinate drawn and labelled where MSB = MSC	1 mark
Marginal external benefit correctly labelled	1 mark
Any other relevant feature of the diagram, e.g. the socially optimal level of consumption labelled on the quantity axis	1 mark per feature up to a maximum of 2 marks

The mark scheme states that 5 or more potential marks can be on offer in a part [03] diagram, of which up to 4 can be awarded.

[04]   Using the data, evaluate the view that because education is a public good, it should always be provided free by the state, and not by private schools. Make sure you include economic arguments in your answer.   (25 marks)

Ⓔ A 'golden rule' to obey when answering part [04] of a data-response question, for which the main skill tested is evaluation, is 'first analyse, then evaluate'. You must build your evaluation on top of relevant and focused analysis in which economic theory is applied to the issue or issues posed by the question.

Good answers to part [04] questions often show evaluation throughout the lines of reasoning pursued as the answer develops. One way to do this is to say, as you introduce each point or argument, whether the point is significant, or whether, though relevant, it is trivial. A conclusion may then attempt to judge the relative strengths of the arguments discussed in the rest of the answer.

Student answer

[01] A subsidy is the opposite of an indirect tax. **a** It is a grant of money by the state to firms in order to reduce the price that consumers have to pay for the goods or services the firms produce. **b** Organisations such as charities can also provide subsidies. **c**

ⓔ **5/5 marks awarded. b** The second sentence in the answer earns all 5 marks. **a** If the answer had been restricted to the first sentence only, 2 marks would have been earned. The question could also be answered in other ways: for example, in terms of the state subsidising consumers directly, e.g. by giving old people bus passes, or a firm cross-subsidising some of its products by using profits made on the more expensive goods it sells to subsidise the loss incurred on goods sold below cost. The answer does mention charities granting subsidies. **c** This sentence on its own would have earned 1 mark.

[02] Whereas only 556,230 pupils attended private schools in 1998, 7,533,470 were taught at state schools. By 2007, the number of private school pupils had increased to 577,670, whereas those attending state schools had fallen to 7,376,170. **a** The reason for this may lie in the fact that the total number of pupils had fallen, which was the result of population decline. **b**

ⓔ **4/8 marks awarded.** This answer only earns half the available marks. The reason is simple: **a** the answer includes only one point of comparison, though the comparison is backed up with evidence from the statistics. To earn full marks for a part [02] answer, you must remember that two points of comparison are needed, together with statistical support. **b** Note also that the student wastes time by drifting into an explanation of the causes of the changes. Part [02] questions never require explanation, though it is a good idea to state why a point of comparison is significant.

[03] The diagram below **a** illustrates why too little education may be provided if the service is only available at unsubsidised market prices.

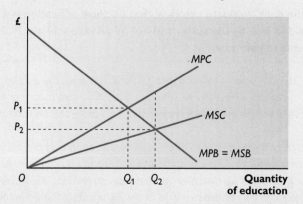

At the unsubsidised market price of P_1, Q_1 education is consumed. **a** The socially optimal level of consumption however is Q_2. **b** This could be achieved if schools price education at P_2. This outcome can be brought about by the government granting schools a subsidy equal to the vertical distance between the *MPC* and the *MSC* curves, above Q_2 on my diagram.

e **10/12 marks awarded.** In this diagram, the positive consumption externality generated when people 'consume' education is depicted as a negative external cost. As a result, the MSC of consuming education is below the MPC. At Q_2, the vertical distance between the MPC and the MSC curves show the MEB of consumption. To earn the 2 marks that have not been awarded, the written explanation needs to be developed, particularly in terms of why the privately optimal level of consumption is Q_1 and the socially optimal level is Q_2.

[04]   I shall begin my answer by disputing the central assertion in the question, namely that education is a public good. **a** Public goods have two characteristics, non-excludability and non-rivalry. On the whole, education does not have either of these characteristics. To take non-rivalry first, the offer of a place to one prospective pupil in a popular state secondary school at the age of eleven may well mean that another pupil who has applied for school entry is not offered a place. In a popular private school, entrance exams are used for pupil selection. Children who don't do well in the exam cannot go to the school. And in the latter case, with regard to non-excludability, children whose parents cannot afford to pay school fees can of course be excluded from the school.

Extract C does of course give examples of elements of education that have public good properties. However, as I have just explained, most education is certainly not a public good, though the public good element is likely to grow. And even for the part of education that may be classified as a public good, free access to education courses (for example through their availability on the internet) does not mean that free marking of essays and coursework can be provided.

There is of course a widely accepted case that education should be provided free by the government, but this is because education is judged to be a merit good rather than a public good. But, even here, there may be a stronger case for subsidised provision in which a price is still charged rather than for completely free provision. The diagram I used in my answer to part [03] of this question illustrates why. **b** If education is provided free and in unlimited quantity, too many people may choose to be educated. Consumption will occur to the right of Q_2 in my diagram, up to the point at which the marginal private benefit (MPB) of education is zero. Over-consumption rather than under-consumption is the result. Additionally, at the margin, people may not value education and the quality of the provided service may be poor.

In conclusion, I believe that, for most children, education should be provided at a price, unsubsidised for richer families, but subsidised for those with lower family incomes. **c** For the very poor, education should be free, but access to the service should be means-tested as family income rises. And because of my right-wing sentiments, **d** I believe that unsubsidised and subsidised provision (for poorer families) via the market, i.e. through private schools, is better than providing education through state schools.

e **21/25 marks awarded.** This is a high-scoring answer, reaching Level 4, but not quite Level 5. The student obviously understands a lot of the relevant economic theory though is somewhat prone to assertion **c** rather than to sufficient development and justification of the points made.

a The answer starts off extremely well by adopting the tactic of 'begging the question' and by providing cogent reasons for doing this. **b** Note also how the student refers to the earlier diagram drawn in the answer to part [03], rather than wasting time by repeating the diagram. Until recently, this was quite a sophisticated ploy, and worth doing provided the reference to the earlier diagram was clearly sign-posted. The ploy was a response to examiners' annoyance at seeing exactly the same diagram drawn several times in one answer. However, in 2010 a new method of marking replaced the traditional method in which a single examiner marked all four parts of your answer to a data-response question. In the new system of screen-based marking, the four parts of your answer are marked online by four different examiners. The examiner marking part [04] will not also mark part [03]. As the examiner won't see the earlier diagram to which you are referring, you may not gain credit for it.

d In the final paragraph the student states a political bias. If reasonable justification is provided for the view expressed, an examiner will probably reward such a stance, even if he or she does not agree with the opinions stated. As a general rule, however, it is best to explore both sides of an argument without necessarily revealing your own political or religious stance (if you have one).

Knowledge check answers

The economic problem

1 Scarcity means there is not enough available of a good to meet demand. Economising means limiting the amount of a scarce good that you will buy and consume so as to be able to buy and consume other goods as well.

2 At this moment, your opportunity cost is the 'next best' thing you could be doing instead of reading this Guide.

Supply and demand in competitive markets

3 Equilibrium is a state of rest or a state of balance between opposing forces. A market is in equilibrium when the amount consumers wish to buy exactly equals the amount producers wish to sell.

4 A shift of demand means the demand curve moves to a new position. An adjustment of demand means that there is an adjustment along the demand curve in response to a change in price.

5 Water is in composite demand since among its many uses are drinking, cooling, heating, cooking and washing.

Elasticity

6 Many people treat table salt as a necessity which must be used in cooking and for scattering on food. There are no close substitutes for table salt, so demand for table salt (as a generic product) is quite price inelastic. However another brand of table salt, say ASDA table salt, is an almost perfect substitute for Tesco's table salt. If Tesco increases the price of Tesco salt but ASDA leaves its price unchanged, some consumers may switch to the cheaper substitute. Demand for Tesco's salt is therefore more price elastic than demand for table salt as a generic product.

7 The plus sign (+) tells us that the good is a *normal good*, i.e. demand for the good increases as income rises. The absolute size of the elasticity statistic (2.3) tells us that demand is income elastic. With this statistic, a 10% increase in income induces a 23% increase in demand. The good is also a *superior good* as well as a normal good. By contrast, an *inferior good* has a negative income elasticity of demand.

8 The minus sign (–) tells us that good A and good B are complementary goods or goods in joint demand. A decrease in the price of good B causes consumers to buy more good B and also increases their demand for the complementary good, good A. The absolute size of the elasticity statistic (0.8) tells us the strength of the joint demand relationship. A 10% decrease in the price of good B leads to an 8% increase in the demand for good A. This is quite a strong joint demand relationship.

Prices and resource allocation

9 The market mechanism and the command mechanism (or planning mechanism) are the two main mechanisms used in economies to try to solve the fundamental economic problem: namely, to allocate scarce resources between competing uses. The market mechanism operates through changes in the relative prices of goods and services, altering the way in which resources are allocated and consumer wants are met. By contrast, in the command mechanism planners make the allocative decisions.

10 A labour market is an example of a factor market, i.e. a market in which the services of a factor of production are bought and sold. Households and firms function simultaneously in both sets of markets, but their roles are reversed. Whereas firms are the source of supply in a goods market, in a factor market firms exercise demand for factor services supplied by households. The incomes received by households from the sale and supply of factor services contribute to households' ability to demand the output supplied by firms in the goods market.

Production and efficiency

11 A business objective is a target or goal which a firm wishes to achieve. Three possible business objectives, other than profit maximisation, are growth maximisation, sales revenue maximisation and output maximisation.

12 The text mentions technical economies of scale and managerial economies of scale. Another type of economy of scale is a bulk-buying economy of scale, which occurs when a firm can buy raw materials at a reduced price when it buys them in large quantities. This is more practical for large firms than for small firms.

Market failure, public goods and externalities

13 A free-rider is somebody who benefits from a good or service without paying. An example is a passerby gaining pleasure from looking at beautiful gardens alongside the footpath she is walking down.

14 Television programmes provide examples of non-pure public goods. BBC and ITV programmes are public goods in the sense that as many people who want to can watch the programmes, providing they have access to a television set. However, broadcasters such as Sky broadcast their programmes as private goods, via satellite and cable. Viewers who are unwilling to pay for the programmes cannot access them — unless they break the law.

15 Marginal cost is the addition to total cost when one extra unit of a good is produced. Average cost (or cost per unit) is total cost divided by the number of units produced. In the context of negative externalities, marginal private cost is the extra cost incurred by a person, for example when buying electricity, marginal external cost is the cost of the extra pollution (negative externality) involved, while marginal social cost (the marginal cost borne by the whole community) is the addition of the marginal private and social costs.

Merit and demerit goods, income and wealth inequalities, and labour immobility

16 Exam students often confuse merit goods with public goods, probably because, if left to markets, under-provision of both results and as a consequence both types of goods are often provided by the government free to consumers. Whereas a public good such as a road is defined by its twin properties of non-excludability and non-rivalry, a merit good such as education can be defined either in terms of externalities generated, or in terms of the information problem.

17 Some pro-free-market economists agree with the libertarian view that people should be allowed to do whatever they want to do — providing they don't harm other people. They reject the concepts of merit goods and demerit goods, arguing that the two concepts legitimise unnecessary interference in people's freedom of choice. The state becomes a 'nanny state'.

18 Equality is a positive term that can be measured. Equity is a normative term based on what is considered to be fair or just.

Monopolies and the allocation of resources

19 Strictly defined, monopoly only exists when there is only one firm in a market or industry (pure monopoly). However, virtually all real-world firms can exercise a degree of monopoly power, though the ability to exercise monopoly power increases the fewer the number of firms in the market. An example of monopoly power is a firm using advertising and/or its brand image to persuade customers to buy its products and not to bother too much about the price they pay.

20 Tap water is supplied through a network of pipelines fed by reservoirs, both of which are owned by the water company serving the local region. Each water company serves a particular river system from which it gets the water it feeds into its reservoirs and pipeline network. For example, Thames Water supplies water to most people living in London. Having two or more water companies serving the same houses and businesses, each with its own storage and distribution system, would be unnecessary duplication which would significantly raise costs. Hence, water companies are natural monopolies.

21 Resources can be misallocated in two main ways. They can be allocated in a productively inefficient way with the result that resources that could be better used elsewhere are tied up in a particular market or industry. Second, they can be inefficiently allocated to consumers, resulting, for example, in under-consumption and hence under-production of merit goods and over-consumption and over-production of demerit goods.

Government intervention in the market

22 In the case of a pure public good such as national defence, it is impossible to provide the good to one person without the rest of society also benefiting. This property of 'non-excludability' means that people can free-ride, benefiting from the good without paying. If too many people choose to free-ride, the incentive function of prices breaks down and it becomes impossible to operate a market.

23 A price ceiling, or maximum legal price, has no effect on a market, providing it is set at a level above the equilibrium price in the market. However, if the price ceiling is imposed *below* the equilibrium price then, provided it is enforced and policed, it will distort the market. Excess demand is created which, in the absence of the price ceiling, would disappear as the price rises towards equilibrium. However, enforcement of the price ceiling prevents this happening. Queues or waiting lists result. These can then lead to the emergence of an illegal secondary market or black market.

24 The most extreme form of regulation is to make it illegal to emit an externality such as pollution. Lesser forms of regulation are restrictions on time of day or year when it is legal to emit the externality, maximum emission limits, and forcing polluters to invest in clean technology.

25 Prices provide information that allows all the traders in the market to plan and co-ordinate their economic activities. This is the signalling function of prices. The information signalled by changing relative prices creates incentives for people to alter their economic behaviour. This is the incentive function of prices.